JAGUAR
WORLD CHAMPIONS

Andrew Whyte

Silk Cut
6
Castrol
JAGUAR
DUNLOP

JAGUAR
WORLD CHAMPIONS

Andrew Whyte

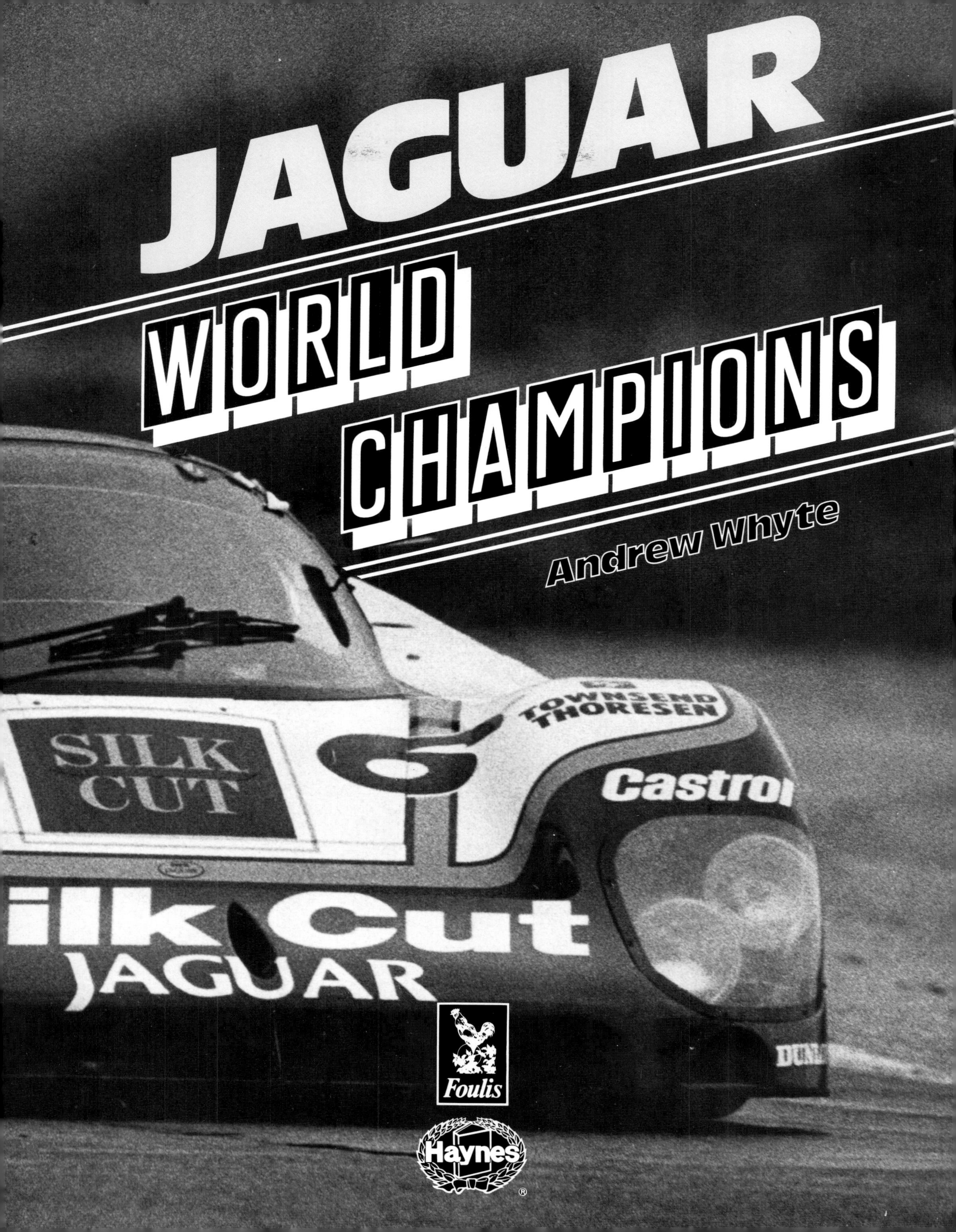

Foulis
Haynes

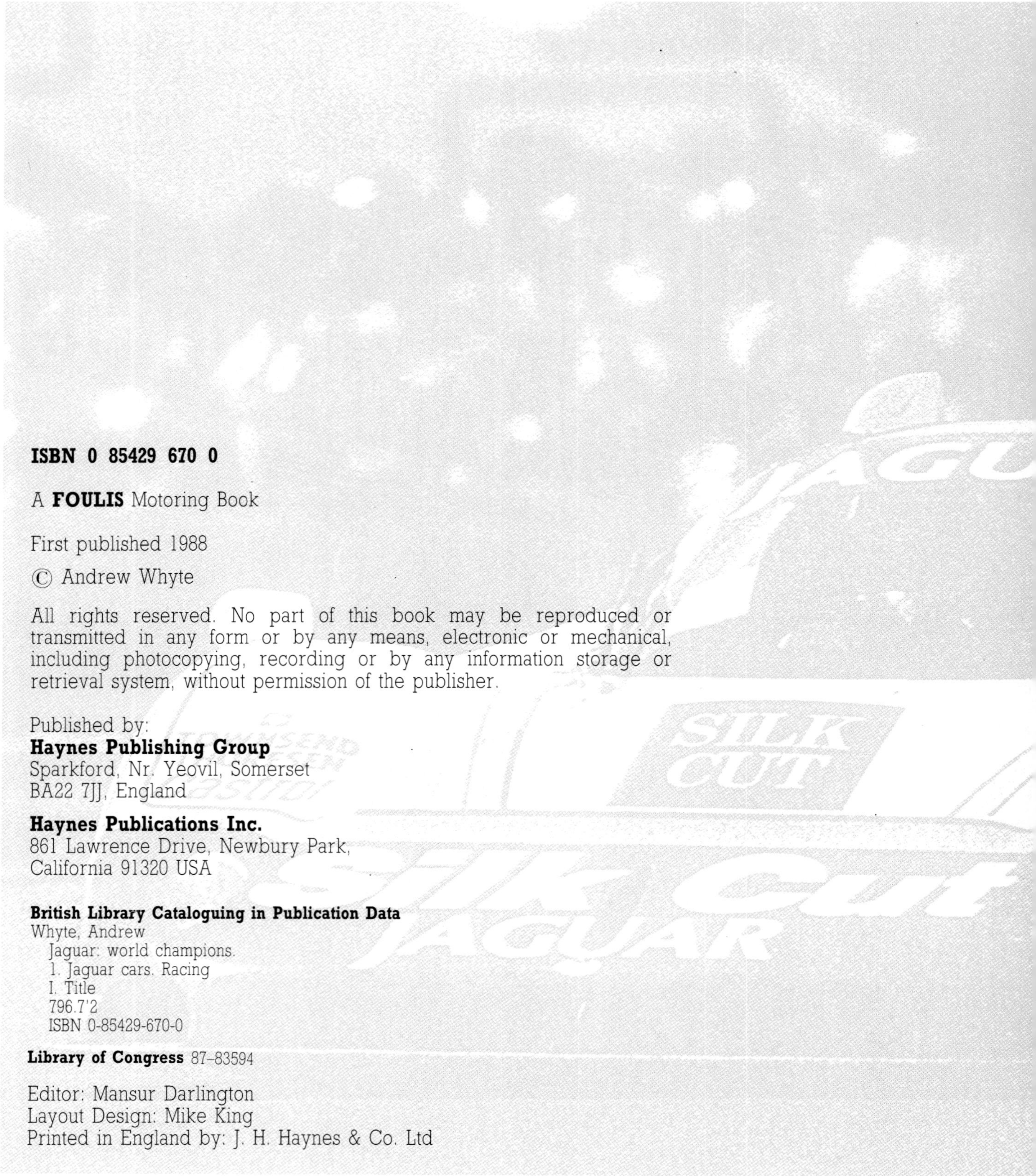

ISBN 0 85429 670 0

A **FOULIS** Motoring Book

First published 1988

Published by:
Haynes Publishing Group
Sparkford, Nr. Yeovil, Somerset
BA22 7JJ, England

Haynes Publications Inc.
861 Lawrence Drive, Newbury Park,
California 91320 USA

British Library Cataloguing in Publication Data
Whyte, Andrew
Jaguar: world champions.
1. Jaguar cars. Racing
I. Title
796.7'2
ISBN 0-85429-670-0

Library of Congress 87-83594

Editor: Mansur Darlington
Layout Design: Mike King
Printed in England by: J. H. Haynes & Co. Ltd

CONTENTS

Foreword

Sports cars – originally those light, manoeuvrable Spyders, now ultra-fast high-performance machines – have always found special favour at Porsche.

The attraction of such highly-developed sports-racing cars lies in their unique combination of maximum performance with extreme durability, which must be sufficient for up to twenty-four hours at racing speeds. It would be hard to present a racing team with a more complete challenge – especially while retaining ties to production sports cars in some areas.

The 1987 season made it clear how exciting endurance races can be, when several manufacturers of equal standing, bearing traditional names, face one another.

Following a long Porsche hegemony, there is a new champion from Jaguar. Once again, we want to extend our hearty congratulations to Jaguar and TWR at this time.

The technical standards, the development tempo, and the professional approach in today's Sports Prototype World Championship are outstanding.

And there is a further factor that impresses me: Although unfortunately no longer true universally, and despite the toughness of the competition, FAIRNESS – on the race track, in pit and paddock, between mechanics, drivers, and team managers – still has a high priority in THIS type of racing.

Peter Falk

Peter Falk
Competitions Director
Dr. Ing.h.c.F. Porsche AG, Stuttgart

Introduction

When I worked at Jaguar I was frequently asked about a return to motor racing.

The works racing team had been effectively disbanded at the 1957 Sebring 12-hour race (then still a World Championship round), but the company continued to support successful private teams, in particular those of Briggs Cunningham in the USA and David Murray *(Ecurie Ecosse)* in the UK. Indeed, the Scottish team's 1957 victory at Le Mans – Jaguar's fifth – was with an ex-works car powered by a factory engine.

From then until 1964, Jaguar supported touring and GT events; but racing development was taking second place to production car development. Jaguar's competitions department was always integral with Jaguar Engineering, and when there was no racing the skills of those involved were channelled to other projects, all of which were, ultimately, related to the XJ series of road cars. The XJ13 mid-engined car, rightly

Friends and rivals: *Peter Falk and Tom Walkinshaw on the day the team championship laurels passed from Porsche to Jaguar.*

admired as an engineering milestone, remained a serious project only until the first Jaguar board meeting after the company's merger with BMC in the summer of 1966, when it was shelved. From then on, it was fairly easy to justify Jaguar's continued abstention, especially when the XJ6 and XJ12 came on to the market, for they signified a distinct change of image for the marque. When British Leyland and Broadspeed went racing with the XJ12 in the 1970s, it was as contrary to good Jaguar marketing as it would be to let the XJ40 loose in some official racing guise today. Nevertheless, the BL/Broadspeed exercise did make one thing quite clear: there is a wealth of popular support for Jaguar when it is seen to go racing. Trying *without winning* was never enough for Jaguar, however.

By the time Jaguar regained its independence under (Sir) John Egan, the face of motor sport, as of industry, had changed completely. In-house race-car preparation had been a thing of the past since Ford showed the modern way to win Le Mans in the late 1960s. To be effective in the modern world, one needed external funding and a specialist engineering department – probably external, too. Although there are close links with Jaguar, the new racing programme is under the control of an independent company, Tom Walkinshaw Racing Ltd. Through administrative agility and specialist knowledge TWR has enabled Jaguar to attain heights of success to which it could not have aspired on its own in the time available. The Southgate-designed Jaguar V12-powered XJR-6 was conceived in late 1984; it first ran in Summer 1985 and within a year had won its first race. In updated (XJR-8) form it won eight of 1987's Sports Prototype World Championship races and took two world titles. This meant entering the domain of the mighty Porsche, the one marque that had retained a close affinity with sports car racing throughout its development in good times and bad.

In 1951, when Jaguar won Le Mans for the first time, a little 1,100cc Porsche won its class there; and the marque continued to prove its reliability year after year. Not until 1970, however, did Porsche win Le Mans outright; by then it had made twenty-five of its incredible flat-12 917s. In 1987, Porsche won Le Mans for the twelfth time. Le Mans is *the* race which Jaguar wanted to win again, more than any other. It was in the minds of all involved, on both sides of the Atlantic, when Jaguar returned to sports car racing in the 1980s. Group 44 tried twice; then TWR tried twice. In 1988, Le Mans remained the unwritten yet absolute priority, and TWR was expected to launch its strongest offensive yet seen at the Sarthe . . .

In 1987, while looking for its elusive sixth Le Mans victory, the Jaguar team made alternative history by winning all but one of the other nine World Championship events – most of them being 1000 km races – to become undisputed champions in the teams and the drivers competitions. Whatever the future holds for Jaguar in racing, 1987 will go down as a very special year. It is close on a decade since I left Jaguar at a time when the marque's whole future was in jeopardy. One reason for leaving was to write books: but not in my wildest dreams did I expect that I should ever be able to entitle one of them *Jaguar – World Champions.* The success of the XJR-8 has, of course, made dreams come true for all the people who used to ask: When is Jaguar coming back? And of course it has made them come true for a whole new generation, too.

As 1988 dawned, TWR was embarking not only on the defence of its world title but on a complete IMSA programme. The International Motor Sports Association had developed a prestigious series for sports-prototypes similar to those raced in the Group C (world) series. Certain details such as wheel sizes and fuel capacities differed, as did the permitted weight; in 1988 there was also to be a 6-litre top limit for non-turbocharged IMSA cars. For the two series, Tony Southgate developed variations on his V12 Jaguar-engined design, known as the XJR-9. While Jaguar reigned supreme in Group C, Porsche's 962 had continued to dominate IMSA, led by Al Holbert on behalf of Stuttgart; and it was a Holbert team driver, Chip Robinson, formerly of the Jaguar North American team run by Bob Tullius, who took the 1987 Camel GT drivers' crown. With new sponsorship, however, Jaguar and TWR looked set to tilt at *this* Porsche pedestal. This book was due to appear as the 1988 season got under way, the XJR-9 having shown its paces on both sides of the ocean. Judging by the eager anticipation, the spirit of sports-car racing was alive and well . . . the word SPORT being totally applicable.

Andrew Whyte
Ettington, England,

'If it's not difficult, it's not worth winning.' – Sir John Egan, Jaguar Chairman and Chief Executive, Silk Cut/Castrol press conference, RAC, London, 14 January 1988.

Author's Acknowledgements

Jaguar and TWR have been very co-operative in making this book possible. At Jaguar Cars Ltd, David Boole, Peter Dodd, Ron Elkins, Alan Hodge, Ian Norris, and Roger Putnam have been most helpful, as have Mike Dale and Mike Cook of Jaguar Cars Inc., New Jersey. Their appointed photographers Richard Bailey, Malcolm Bryan, and Hal Crocker have helped me overcome many of the problems of photographing people and events around the world.

Tom Walkinshaw, Roger Silman, Paul Davis, Allan Scott, Jeremy Russ and the whole TWR team have been encouraging to me, and I'm also grateful to the many drivers of past and present TWR Jaguar teams who have given me their time. One in particular should be quoted *(from Page 328 of my book Jaguar Sports Racing and Works Competition Cars):* "Porsche will recover", Brian Redman said, several years ago. "Porsche has forgotten more about racing than most manufacturers ever knew. They are racing bred. The whole factory has been oriented towards racing for twenty years."

Porsche *will* recover. In any case, there are many fields in which it remains undefeated. And in defeat, it is gracious. I am delighted that Peter Falk agreed to provide the Foreword to this book which is, above all, the story of Jaguar's success. His sportsmanlike attitude does not alter his resolve to provide Jaguar's Silk Cut and Castrol sponsored racing teams with the strong competition that will ensure the survival and the success of sports car racing at the highest level. I would also thank, in advance, the other teams that will, surely, challenge both Porsche and Jaguar, to keep them on their toes.

1

JAGUAR – WORLD CHAMPIONS 1987

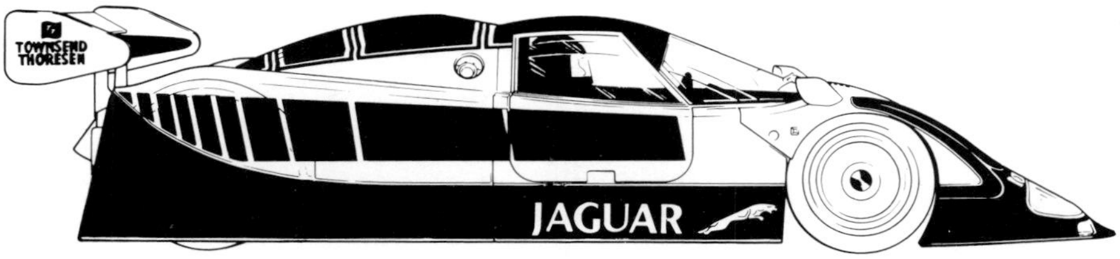

That was, rightly, the claim of Jaguar's advertising. Simplicity is the keynote of any commercial claim to fame, and Jaguar had just joined an illustrious role of honour – although, technically, the claim was invalid since the manufacturers' championship had been abolished after 1984, in favour of a championship for teams. Because of this, I make no excuse for using the original marking system to illustrate the inter-marque battle which brought Jaguar so much success in the thirty-fifth year of The World Sports Car Championship.

In 1950 the Formula One World Championship was inaugurated for drivers only; Grand Prix car manufacturers would not be recognised separately until 1958. In 1953, however, the sporting commission of the FIA *(Fédération Internationale de l' Automobile)* introduced what was officially described as the Manufacturers' Championship, and what became known as the World Sports Car Championship. No fewer than five makes won qualifying rounds that year: Aston Martin, Cunningham, Ferrari, Jaguar and Lancia. The Cunningham car, winner of the very first WSC race (Sebring, 1953) did not stay around for long because its manufacture was a bit of patriotism rather than a profit-maker for that fine American sportsman Briggs Cunningham; the other race winners operated as at least partially commercial enterprises. Three of them went on to become WSC champions. The one that did not do so was Jaguar. Preoccupied with Le Mans as a means of promoting itself, the Coventry company did not take much notice of the new 'league table', and private entrants scored most of the points which by chance made Jaguar a very close runner-up to Ferrari.

By the later 1950s Jaguar had achieved its purpose by winning the *Grand Prix d'Endurance* at Le Mans five times. What involvement the marque retained with racing over the next few years was mostly on the

touring car scene – although Jaguar did produce one sports-prototype (the XJ13) in the mid-1960s.

Not until its 1980s revival did Jaguar look at world-class racing as a means of publicity. The WSC had taken many turns in the meantime. Its name had been changed several times and, often, there was a shortage of true competition between makes. This is why the inter-team contest was

An early 1987 picture celebrating the manufacture of 100,000 Jaguar V12 engines in sixteen years of production – mainly for the XJ-S coupé which did much to

The Tony Southgate-designed TWR-built Silk Cut Jaguar Team XJR-8, winner of eight of 1987's World Championship sports car races.

The Heart of a Champion. The naturally aspirated Jaguar V12 engine, originated by Walter Hassan and Harry Mundy in the 1960s, produced for sophisticated road cars since the early 1970s, and seen here as adapted for TWR Jaguar Racing by Allan Scott and his engineers at Kidlington to win the 1987 World Sports Car Championship.

maintain Jaguar's sporting image after the E-type had gone. Also shown is the Design Council Award-winning XJR-6, painted in 1987 livery (as for the XJR-8).

introduced in 1985 – ironically the year in which the Jaguar Group C car appeared. As Ferrari had dominated the early years of the championship, so Porsche often found itself monopolising the scene at this stage.

Back in the early days, there had been a simple marking system: points for the top six places in the general classification of a race were valued 8, 6, 4, 3, 2, and 1 respectively – but only *one* example of any marque could score. Although the races of 1987 saw up to a dozen turbocharged Porsche 962s taking on two or three Jaguars, application of the old system shows that Jaguar was at last the champion marque in anyone's language, thus:

Race	**Jaguar v.**	**Porsche**
Jarama	8	6
Jerez	8	6
Monza	8	6
Silverstone	8	4
Le Mans	2	8
Norisring	3	8
Brands Hatch	8	6
Nürburgring	8	6
Francorchamps	8	4
Fuji	8	4
Total (old) points	**69**	**58**

Porsche and Jaguar are great names in their own right, with different and highly individual approaches to motor sports.

One thing they have in common is the desire to see the World Sports Car Championship retain its title and be worthy of it. No matter how many promotional problems there were all round them in 1987, the Porsche teams and the Silk Cut Jaguar Team conducted their duel in a totally dedicated and professional manner. Although the Lancia LC2 rarely appeared (due to the Italian company's preoccupation with rallying), 1987 was notable for the emergence of potential competition from France and Japan. Especially impressive, too, was the Swiss-German effort. Sponsored by Kouros for a second season, the Sauber-Mercedes failed to score a victory (except for one in the German Supercup series) but its technical merit and its performance in only five WSC events made it clear that Mercedes-Benz – like Jaguar – was itching to relive its former glories.

Such a variety of famous makes competing for international honours – in the spriit of the original championship for sports-racing cars – may make life even more difficult for Porsche. But that is the kind of challenge that will make the racing better still . . .

And the next challenge for Jaguar, now that it had reached this goal? When these words were written, before the 1988 season, Porsche still held the ace most coveted by Jaguar; the ace which Jaguar had held five times before, a generation ago. Now Jaguar wanted it back, more than any other sporting honour . . . Le Mans.

Champion marques 1953-1987

1987	**JAGUAR**
1982 to 1986	Porsche
1980 and 1981	Lancia
1978 and 1979	Porsche
1977	Alfa Romeo
1976	Porsche
1975	Alfa Romeo
1973 and 1974	Matra-Simca
1972	Ferrari
1969 to 1971	Porsche
1968	Ford
1967	Ferrari
1966	Ford
1960 to 1965	Ferrari
1959	Aston Martin
1956 to 1958	Ferrari
1955	Mercedes-Benz
1953 and 1954	Ferrari

Theoretical winners are shown where no single marque was champion, ie, in 1962, 1963, 1977 and since 1985.

Top Team

Although Porsche AG made mid-season news by withdrawing its one team from the last four races of 1987, there was no loss of competition for the Silk Cut Jaguar Team on a race-by-race basis.

Porsche had its reasons for pulling out, and these certainly did NOT imply a reduced interest in motor racing: quite the contrary, in fact. Traditionally, Jaguar would re-assess its programme after it had won Le Mans – the most charismatic race on the world calendar – and Porsche's decision to do the same thing was understandable in view of the heavy programme it had set itself in other fields of competition. Moreover, its policy of serving its racing customers meant that several teams running Porsche's 962 Group C car were perfectly capable of taking the title.

True, 1985 had seen the works Porsche team win the first Teams' Championship handsomely from Lancia and four private Porsche users: Joest, Kremer, Lloyd and Brun. The fledgling Castrol-assisted Jaguar team had been seventh overall. In 1986, the Rothmans-backed Porsches had shared third place with the Silk Cut Jaguar team, both beaten by Brun and Joest – so it was still, in effect, Porsches all the way.

In 1987, the Silk Cut Jaguar Team began as it meant to go on: by

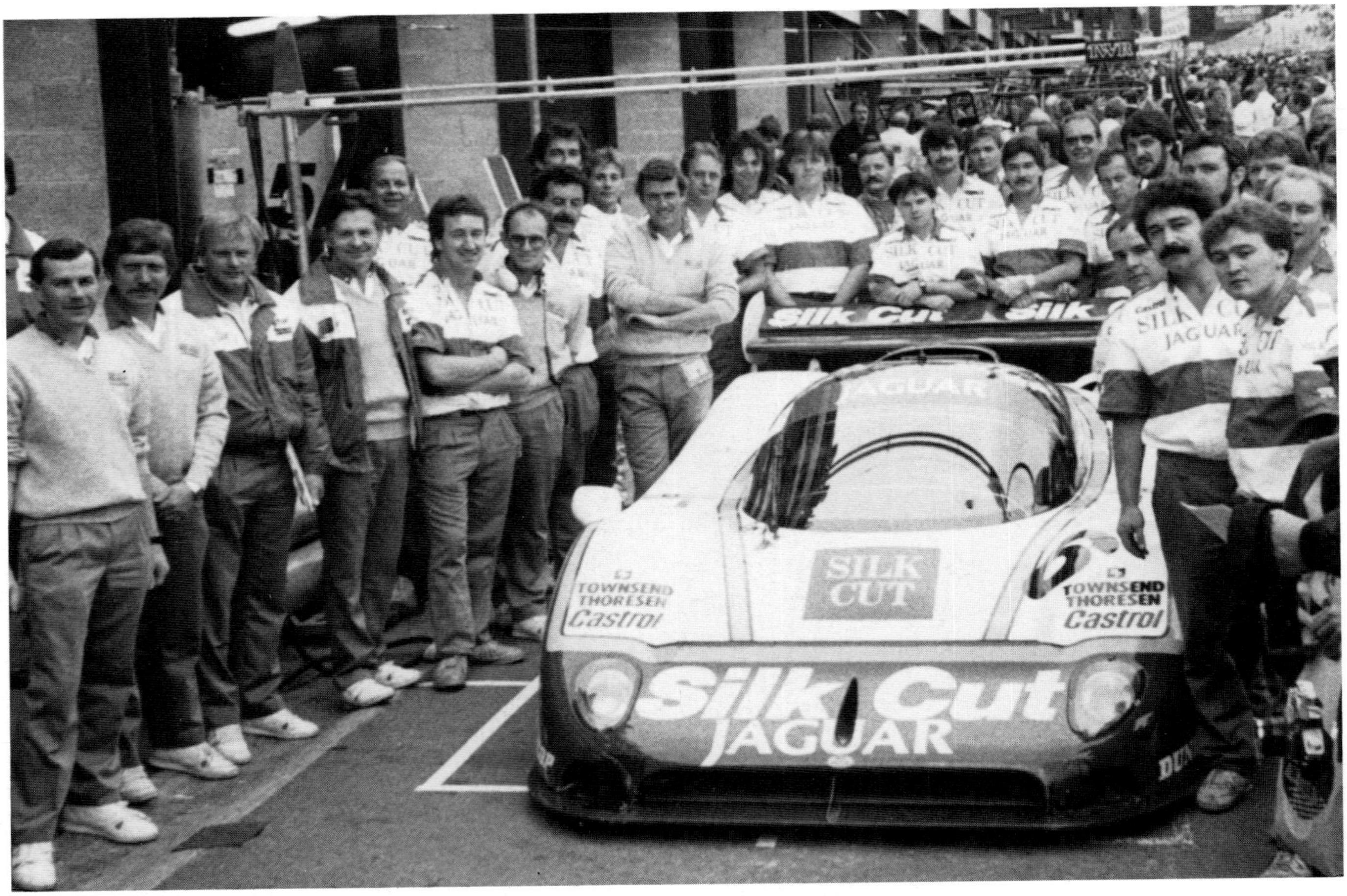

The team of '87: seen with the car which they have just rebuilt for the second time, and which is about to win the title-clinching race in Belgium, are **from left** *Manager Paul Davis, Power Unit Engineer Allan Scott, Director Roger Silman, Designer Tony Southgate and their magnificent team of race engineers and fitters.*

Sir John Egan, architect of Jaguar's reconstruction in the 1980s, reckons his presence has brought ill-luck on the TWR team several times. Not so at Spa-Francorchamps in September 1987, when he witnessed his marque winning its second world title in a fortnight – a victory masterminded by TWR director and race team chief Roger Silman, here with Egan on the starting grid.

winning. Two standard cars showed that they were equally capable of winning, and when a third car was brought in – for Silverstone, Le Mans and (especially) Spa-Francorchamps – it proved a great asset to the team's race strategy. Victory in the team championship was a probability at Brands Hatch and a certainty at the Nürburgring, where Porsche motor sport chief Peter Falk produced a bottle of champagne to toast his rivals. By Round Nine, therefore, Walter Brun had conceded his team crown to the Silk Cut Jaguars, run for Tom Walkinshaw Racing Limited by Roger Silman.

A nice touch in Belgium was the public handing-over of the teams' world title by 1986 winner Walter Brun of Switzerland **(right)** *to Tom Walkinshaw and Sir John Egan. The German-based Brun Porsches came second to Jaguar in 1987, with Porsche AG third.*

It could be argued that the twin-turbocharged Porsche 962C was becoming obsolete, despite continual development of new features such as anti-lock braking and the PDK (double clutch) transmission by the works. On the other hand, it was also apparent that the freedom of privateers to engineer their own ideas into the basic 962 design was keeping it young. The Silverstone-based single-car team of John Britten and Richard Lloyd proved this more than any other, and was rewarded with the year's only privateer victory at WSC level.

There was a slice of the action for most of the serious runners but, in the end, the result was clearcut: Jaguar first – Porsche second, third, fourth, fifth and sixth – *see table overleaf.*

Team Championship table, 1987

	Silk Cut Jaguar Team (Britain)	Brun Motorsport, Porsche (Switzerland)	Porsche AG (West Germany)	Joest Racing Porsche (W. Germany)	Britten -Lloyd, Porsche (Britain)	Kremer Porsche (West Germany)
Jarama	20	8	15	–	3	10
Jerez	20	6	12	–	–	15
Monza	20	12	15	10	–	–
Silverstone	20	8	12	–	–	–
Le Mans	8	–	20	–	–	10
Norisring	10	15	–	12	20	–
Brands Hatch	20	8	–	10	15	6
Nürburgring	20	12	–	15	8	–
Francorchamps	20	12	–	8		–
Fuji	20	10	–	8	12	–
Total Points:	178	91	74	63	58	41
Final Position	**1st**	2nd	3rd	4th	5th	6th

Only one car per team scores in any race, and all ten results count (no deletions). Points/Position: 20/1st, 15/2nd, 12/3rd, 10/4th, 8/5th, 6/6th, 4/7th, 3/8th, 2/9th, 1/10th.

The Driver's Championship

A series of planned changes (for the late 1980s and the 1990s) suggested that sports-prototype racing might continue to evolve in a way that should appeal to motor manufacturers. The future of Group C is referred to in a later chapter.

One change, which made sense, was the introduction as early as 1988 of a new scale of points accumulation. For 'sprint' events (360 km races, as for Jarama and Norisring in 1987, and planned for Jarama and Brno in 1988) the regular marking system would be used. For normal-length races (800 – 1000 km) the points would be doubled, however, and for Le Mans they were to be tripled. It has often been said (in Group A as well as Group C) that such a sliding scale would reflect championship positions better.

As can be seen from the 1987 WSC drivers' table, the regular Jaguar drivers took the top four places. It is therefore interesting to note that Derek Bell and Hans-Joachim Stuck would have been second and third (instead of fifth and sixth) if 1988's points system had been applied to 1987. It would have resulted in the following order:

1st Boesel, 254 points; 2nd Bell, 204; 3rd Stuck, 204; 4th Cheever, 186; 5th = Lammers and Watson, 184.

The foregoing, however, did *not* apply in 1987 which, nevertheless, witnessed several changes of leader before Raul Boesel established

Raul Boesel with TWR's engineer in charge of car No.4, Alastair McQueen.

The regular driver team meets the press at Round One, Jarama 1987. Left to right are Ron Elkins (just visible), *John Watson, Eddie Cheever, Jaguar's PR Manager for Europe Ian Norris, Raul Boesel and Jan Lammers.*

himself as the champion-elect. Despite the initial advantage of Jaguar over Porsche, the winnings were being shared between the Jaguar pairs (Lammers/Watson and Cheever/Boesel) while Porsche AG's reigning champions Bell and Stuck were consistently well-placed. Lammers/Watson led after Round One at Jarama; Cheever/Boesel took over at Jerez; but after Round Three at Monza Bell and Stuck were ahead. Lammers and Watson went one point in front of the Porsche drivers after Silverstone; but at Le Mans the latter pair went ahead again with a superbly-judged win which depended upon a long fuel-saving pace-car period – an audacious gamble which was rewarded in full.

Of the Jaguar drivers, Eddie Cheever's chances were reduced because, as a Grand Prix driver, he had to miss three races due to the clash of dates: Monza, Brands Hatch, and Fuji. He had to count every result.

For Round Nine, in Belgium, there were three cars and seven drivers to make sure of the championship. From left, they were Martin Brundle (UK), Raul Boesel (Brazil), Johnny Dumfries (UK), Eddie Cheever (USA), John Watson (UK), John Nielsen (Denmark) and Jan Lammers (Netherlands).

1987 World Sportscar Champion, Raul Boesel, winner of five races out of ten.

He would end the season with no 'spare' points to delete whereas his substitute, John Nielsen, helped Boesel recover from an early mistake to win Round Seven at Brands Hatch. That was the turning point, Boesel taking a lead which he would never lose. However, at Nürburgring for Round Eight, Bell and Stuck finished second, and were still close behind with 99 points to Boesel's 110. Jaguar had the team title, but the drivers' prize was still not quite watertight.

To make absolutely sure that nothing could go wrong, Tom Walkinshaw sent three XJR-8s for Round Nine, the 1000 km race at Spa-Francorchamps in the Belgian Ardennes. Cheever was back on strength, with Nielsen in Jaguar No. 4; Lammers and Watson drove No. 5 as usual; No. 6 was an extra car for Martin Brundle and Johnny Dumfries, two of Britain's hungrier young lions. Key to the plan was to nominate Boesel for all three cars, then put him in the car that looked most promising. The plan worked perfectly; driving No. 6, Boesel won, and put himself in an unassailable position. If it had been known that there was to be only one race in Japan instead of two, then that little exercise in Belgium would have been unnecessary. As it was, Fuji – the tenth and final round – made quite sure that Jaguar drivers filled the leaderboard down to fourth place:

Driver's Championship table 1987

The Top Four Jaguar Drivers

	Raul Boesel (Brazil)	Jan Lammers (Netherlands)	John Watson (Britain)	Eddie Cheever (USA)
Jarama	12	20	20	12
Jerez	20	–	–	20
Monza	–	20	20	–
Silverstone	20	15	15	20
Le Mans	(8)	–	–	8
Norisring	(10)	–	–	10
Brands Hatch	20	12	12	–
Nürburgring	20	–	–	20
Francorchamps	20	15	15	10
Fuji	15	20	20	–
Total Points	(145)	102	102	100
Best seven	127	102	102	100
Final position	**1st**	= 2nd	= 2nd	4th

The Top Four Porsche Drivers

	Derek Bell (Britain)	Hans-J Stuck (Germany)	Oscar Larrauri (Argentina)	Mauro Baldi (Italy)
Jarama	15	15	8	3
Jerez	12	12	4	–
Monza	15	15	–	–
Silverstone	12	12	–	–
Le Mans	20	20	–	20
Norisring	–	–	15	20
Brands Hatch	10	10	8	15
Nürburgring	15	15	12	8
Francorchamps	(8)	(8)	12	–
Fuji	(6)	–	10	12
Total Points	(113)	(107)	69	58
Best seven	99	99	69	58
Final position	5th	6th	7th	8th

Driver must complete 30 per cent of race to score; best seven results count.
points position 20/1st, 15/2nd, 12/3rd, 10/4th, 8/5th, 6/6th, 4/7th, 3/8th, 2/9th, 1/10th.

Past champions: (all Porsche drivers) were John Paul Senior, USA (1980); Bob Garretson, USA (1981); Jacky Ickx, Belgium (1982 and 1983); Stefan Bellof, Germany (1984); Derek Bell, Britain, and Hans-Joachim Stuck, Germany (1985); and Derek Bell (1986).

2

JAGUAR V PORSCHE

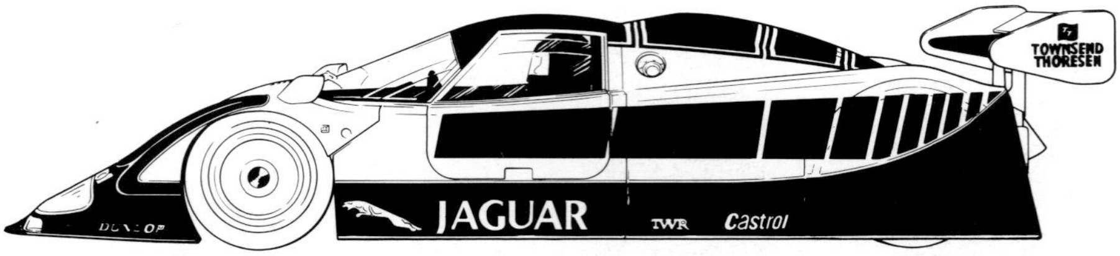

The Group C Story

The World Sports Car Championship was started in 1953, and it has maintained an unbroken record into the Group C era.

From the outset, it was difficult to define a sports-*racing* car, since one set of viewpoints was related to the production car and the other to meeting the race regulations in the way most likely to bring victory. For example, there were different interpretaions of a two-seater body: With their D-type, Jaguar put in a second seat – but access to it was via something akin to a manhole. A passenger *could* sit there, at a pinch. When organisers carped, a compromise was reached by cutting out a small section of the body, to make a hole where the door might have been, and then screwing the section back on. A little later came the windscreen-dimension rules, which led to the 1958-style Lister and the 'birdcage' Maserati. Safety controls – especially in the specification and handling of fuel, and in terms of engine power output – have been similarly hard to apply.

After a very uncertain period, during which the championship's aims were lost in a mixture of 'GT' and 'prototype' categories, sports car racing re-emerged as a modern formula within fundamentally simple parameters. Group C (for 'two-seater competition automobiles built specially for races on closed circuits') was introduced for the 1982 racing season.

As regards the power unit, freedom of choice was almost complete from the outset, as long as the engine ran on normal petrol (up to 102 RON)

Jaguar v Porsche
The story of 1987: Jaguar won both championships, but Porsche won Le Mans. This book went to press before the 1988 season got under way; but it was a season which promised maximum effort from both these great teams at Le Mans – Porsche aiming to maintain their domination, Jaguar determined to regain the greatest title in sports-car racing.

and was 'recognised by a manufacturer who has already homologated cars in Group A or B'. The only limiting factor was fuel consumption and, although the situation improved each year, some of the early races were badly affected by contenders having to slow to unreasonably low speeds in order to finish. As with Formula One in the same period, fuel efficiency

The two Jaguar men most directly involved with the racing programme are engineering director Jim Randle (left) *whose new Whitley, Coventry, technical centre provides testing and quality-assurance facilities for TWR, and Mike Dale:* (right), *second-in-command at Jaguar Cars Inc., New Jersey, and responsible for the North American Jaguar racing programmes since 1974.*

got better and better (and easier for the driver to calculate) as experience of this aspect increased.

The fuel tank capacity was limited to 100 litres, and there were prescribed fuel allowances for each race. Each year, however, there would be modifications to these prescriptions. Le Mans in particular was difficult to master, even by Porsche, due to wayward decisions as to the amounts of fuel which could be consumed. In 1985, the fastest C1 cars were expected to survive for 24 hours at Le Mans on only 2210 litres of fuel. The 2550 litres permitted in 1986 and 1987 – the first two years of TWR participation – made more sense. For the most common race distance of 1000 km, 510 litres was the ration.

Another restriction was a rate of flow of 60 litres per minute when refuelling.

The minimum weight of any C1 car was set at 850 kg from 1985 (800 kg having been permitted earlier). Maximum exterior dimensions of 480 cm by 200 cm by 110 cm were supplemented by other criteria such as proportions of overhang, windscreen height and ground effect. One of the later Group C rule changes – picked up from the American IMSA regulations – specified that the driver's footwell must be placed aft of the theoretical front axle line. Porsche had created their 962 to meet that IMSA requirement, anyway. Maximum tyre width was set at 19 inches.

Cars to the old Group 6 regulations were allowed to race in 1982, but they were not eligible for points in the Championship of Makes.

Parallel with C1, Group C2 (formerly Group C Junior) developed into a worthwhile and competitive formula. The battles between the two British teams of Gordon Spice and Hugh McCaig *(Ecurie Ecosse)* raged from 1985 throughout 1987. C2 worked on the same principle as C1, with lower weight and fuel figures. By contrast, as a racing formula, the Group B idea did not get off the ground.

As the highly competitive 1987 Group C season drew to a close, new plans and new hopes were countered by new fears.

The teams arrived in Japan anticipating two races: an endurance event at Fuji and a 360 km 'sprint' at Sendai. They were greeted with the information that the latter had been cancelled, and it was only natural for them to feel utterly let down – for their sponsorship negotiations had been based on there being two events. If the Nishi-Sendai circuit was not up to scratch – and it was not – then why had there not been any warning? The answer proved to be a matter of trust: trust in the belief that the work *would* be done and, therefore, that there was no need to tell anyone there was a problem (in case of panic?). After all, if there had been no race in Japan there would have been no Group C championship race outside Europe. So, was the *World* championship status at risk?

Perhaps so. The very first WSC series in 1953 had consisted of seven rounds, including the Sebring 12-hour race and the Carrera Panamericana Mexico; and there had been several non-European races in most series ever since. Thirty years later, in 1983, there were 1000 km races at Fuji in Japan, and Kyalami in South Africa. In 1984 four of the eleven races were outside Europe: one each in Africa, Australia, Canada, and Japan. In 1985 there were three (Canada, Japan, and Malaysia) out of ten. In 1986 and 1987 – after some cancellations – the geography of Group C looked a little

Jaguar's first and only in-house mid-engined racing car was the Browns Lane-built 5-litre 4ohc XJ13. It never raced, but it lapped the MIRA circuit at over 160 mph back in 1967 driven by David Hobbs. Jaguar's chief experimental test engineer, Norman Dewis, was photographed at the wheel by Andrew Whyte.

The modern mid-engined Jaguar, designed by Tony Southgate and built by TWR with the full co-operation and on behalf of Jaguar Cars Ltd. No.4 is the 1987 World Sports-Prototype Championship-winning XJR-8 and No.6 is the Le Mans variation of it. Readers of Britain's AUTOSPORT *weekly voted the Jaguar XJR-8 'Racing Car of the Year' for 1987, ahead of the Williams and Ferrari GP Cars.*

AUTOGLASS
TOWNSEND
THORESEN
6 Silk Cut
JAGUAR
TWR
DUNLOP
Castrol
DUNLOP

AUTOGLASS
TOWNSEND
THORESEN
4 Silk Cut
JAGUAR
TWR Castrol DUNLOP
DUNLOP

sparse, with only Fuji remaining of the far-flung venues. 1985 had been a bad season, in that two top drivers, Manfred Winkelhock and Stefan Bellof of Germany, lost their lives at speed in Group C cars – the former at Mosport, Canada, which had proved treacherous on other occasions and was omitted subsequently by general consent. There were tangible reasons for the other changes, too. Yet, once 1987 had lost its planned Australian date, and then one of the Japanese ones, the sports car series was in the firing line yet again.

World-class motor sports have always been controlled from Paris, ever since the birth of the car and of motor racing. Towards the end of 1987, the political nature of it all was demonstrated by the unanimous decision to re-elect France's Jean-Marie Balestre for a further four-year term as President of FISA. His backers included Britain through its representation in the guise of former driver and Brabham team proprietor Bernard Ecclestone; his relatively new role as Balestre's deputy and his enthusiasm for a new championship in 1989 for silhouette cars – specials built to *look* like production models – indicated that his own ambitions came before the development of the traditions of the sport.

The World Sports Car Championship was not dead yet, however, and although the manufacturer's representative, Jürgen Barth, was not re-elected to the FIA sports-prototype commission for 1988, a noteworthy addition was that of John Bishop's IMSA competitions director Mark Raffauf. Group C and IMSA had been looking for ways and means of operating more closely. Perhaps their appointment would help retain a World Series in the long run?

The immediate future of Group C did not involve as many instant changes as had been feared at first. For 1988, the only major alterations were the new and potentially-better scoring system (mentioned earlier in this book) and a requirement for a larger flat area on the underside of the car, together with specific restrictions in tunnelled air-flow.

The same late-1987 FIA meeting stated that from 1989 C1 and C2 minimum-weight limits would go up from 850 to 900 kg and 700 to 750 kg respectively, and non-turbocharged stock-block engines (eg; Jaguar V12) would be restricted to 6.0 litres; and the fuel efficiency formula would go, to be replaced by new turbocharger boost controls – two ideas straight out of IMSA. Turbocharging was to be banned by 1991 when 3.5-litre Formula One-type engines would be allowed, and, before then, a return of the Group B Grand Touring category was being anticipated.

Reactions at the time were varied and, naturally, wary. For the Silk Cut Jaguar Team, Roger Silman went on record as being 'very disappointed', because Tony Southgate and Allan Scott had achieved the existing weight limit only to find that this particular work would no longer be of value. He also indicated that he felt the fuel efficiency formula did work – certainly, he and his team had proved it in 1987 – while Porsche's Peter Falk and Sauber's Max Welti also expressed disappointment, on the basis of the variety and equality of specifications in the three leading C1 contenders. Of course, they all felt that World status was an important attraction for many people and organisations; not least Jaguar, Mercedes Benz, and Porsche – three companies which had no comment to make on the 'Silhouette' production-car idea. It all boiled down to the fact that manufacturers like to continue to develop vehicles along a particular course for as long as they can.

One thing was certain: there *would* be a Sports-Prototype Championship for 1988, with events scheduled to take place in Japan and Australia. As in 1987, there would be just two 'sprints': one at Jarama and one at the Czechoslovakian circuit near Brno (knocking out the controversial Norisring), thus adding a new European country to the WSC list. Apart from these, and Le Mans, all the races were due to run for 1000 km (or six hours). The full list read: Jerez on 6th March, Jarama on 13th March, Monza on 10th April, Silverstone on 8th May, Le Mans on 12/13th June, Brno on 10th July, Brands Hatch on 24th July, Spa-Francorchamps on 28th August, Nürburgring on 4th September, Fuji on 9th October and Sandown Park, Melbourne on 20th November, although there seemed to be an element of cry-wolf there. There was also talk of a Group C/IMSA match race in America the following week.

At the time of writing, after six seasons of the formula there had been fifty-eight Group C championship races, forty of them going to Porsche cars. After the domination by Porsche, however, it was interesting to note the new balance of power during the 1986 and 1987 seasons: Out of nineteen races Porsche and Jaguar had nine victories each, with the remaining event going to the Mercedes-powered Sauber. The presence of those three great names alone seemed to guarantee another fine season in 1988 – whatever else the long-term future might hold for the racing sports car.

This section concludes with a full list of winners from 1982 to 1987.

Group C: the Winners, 1982 – 1987

1982 Race Winners in World Endurance Championship

Monza 1000 km	18 April	Pescarolo/Rondeau/Francia (Rondeau-C.)
Silverstone 6 hours*	16 May	Alboreto/Patrese (Lancia)
Nürburgring 1000 km*	30 May	Alboreto/Patrese (Lancia)
Le Mans 24 hours	19/20 June	Ickx/Bell (Porsche 956)
Spa-F'champs 1000 km	5 Sept	Ickx/Mass (Porsche 956)
Mugello 1000 km*	19 Sept	Alboreto/Ghinzani (Lancia)
Fuji 6 hours	3 Oct	Ickx/Mass (Porsche 956)
Brands Hatch 1000 km	17 Oct	Ickx/Bell (Porsche 956)

World Champion: Jacky Ickx (Belgian)
World Champion Make: Porsche

**Drivers' points counted, but Lancia Group 6 cars were not eligible for Championship of Makes.*

1983 Race winners in World and European Championships

Monza 1000 km	10 April	Wollek/Boutsen (Porsche 956)
Silverstone 1000 km	8 May	Bell/Bellof (Porsche 956)
Nürburgring 1000 km	29 May	Ickx/Mass (Porsche 956)
Le Mans 24 hours	18/19 June	Haywood/Holbert/Schuppan (956)
Spa-F'champs 1000 km	4 Sept	Ickx/Mass (Porsche 956)
Brands Hatch 1000 km	18 Sept	Warwick/Fitzpatrick (Porsche 956)
Fuji 1000 km	2 Oct	Bell/Bellof (Porsche 956)
Imola 1000 km	16 Oct	Fabi/Heyer (Lancia LC2)
Mugello 1000 km	23 Oct	Wollek/Johansson (Porsche 956)
Kyalami 1000 km	10 Dec	Bell/Bellof (Porsche 956)

World Champion: Jacky Ickx (Belgian)
European Champion: Bob Wollek (French)
World Champion Make: Porsche

** Races stopped at 6-hour mark*

1984 Race winners in World Endurance Championship

Monza 1000 km	23 April	Bell/Bellof (Porsche 956)
Silverstone 1000 km	13 May	Ickx/Mass (Porsche 956)
Le Mans 24 hours	16/17 June	Ludwig/Pescarolo (Porsche 956)
Neue N'gring 1000 km*	15 July	Bell/Bellof (Porsche 956)
Brands Hatch 1000 km	29 July	Lammers/Palmer (Porsche 956)
Mosport 1000 km	5 Aug	Ickx/Mass (Porsche 956)
Spa-F' 1000 km	2 Sept	Bell/Bellof (Porsche 956)
Imola 1000 km	16 Sept	Bellof/Stuck (Porsche 956)
Fuji 1000 km	30 Sept	Bellof/Watson (Porsche 956)
Kyalami 1000 km	3 Nov	Patrese/Nannini (Lancia LC2)
Sandown 1000 km	2 Dec	Bell/Bellof (Porsche 956)

World Champion: Stefan Bellof (German)
World Champion Make: Porsche

** Race stopped at 6-hour mark*

1985 Race winners in World Endurance Championship

Mugello 6 hours	14 April	Ickx/Mass (Porsche 962)
Monza 1000 km	28 April	Winkelhock/Surer (Porsche 962)
Silverstone 1000 km	12 May	Ickx/Mass (Porsche 962)
Le Mans 24 hours	15/16 June	Ludwig/Barilla/"Winter" (956)
Hockenheim 1000 km	14 July	Bell/Stuck (Porsche 962)
Mosport 1000 km	11 Aug	Bell/Stuck (Porsche 962)

Spa-F'champs 1000 km†	1 Sept	Baldi/Patrese/Wollek (Lancia LC2)
Brands Hatch 1000 km	22 Sept	Bell/Stuck (Porsche 962)
Fuji 1000 km*	6 Oct	Hoshino (March-Nissan)
Selangor 800 km	1 Dec	Ickx/Mass (Porsche 962)

World Champions: Derek Bell (British) and Hans-Joachim Stuck (German)
World Champion Team: Rothmans Porsche

† Race halted at c.850 km following death of Stefan Bellof
** Race boycotted by leading contenders, and halted at c.275 km due to rain.*

1986 Race winners in World Sports-Prototype Championship

Monza 1000 km	20 April	Bell/Stuck (Porsche 962)
Silverstone 1000 km	5 May	Cheever/Warwick (Jaguar XJR-6)
Le Mans 24 hours	31 May/1 Jun	Bell/Stuck/Holbert (Porsche 962)
Norisring 180 km	29 June	Ludwig (Porsche 962)
Brands Hatch 1000 km	20 July	Wollek/Baldi (Porsche 962)
Jerez 360 km	3 Aug	Larrauri/Pareja (Porsche 962)
Neue N'gring 1000 km*	24 Aug	Thackwell/Pescarolo (S-Mercedes)
Spa-F'champs 1000 km	15 Sept	Boutsen/Jelinski (Porsche 962)
Fuji 1000 km	6 Oct	Barilla/Ghinzani (Porsche 962)

World Champion: Derek Bell (British)†
World Champion Team: Brun Motorsport Porsche

** Race stopped and restarted but shortened to c.550 km*
† Hans-Joachim Stuck scored equal points but was placed second on a technicality.

1987 Race winners in World Sports-Prototype Championship

Jarama, 360 km	22 March	Lammers/Watson (Jaguar XJR-8)
Jerez 6-hour	29 March	Boesel/Cheever (Jaguar XJR-8)
Monza 1000 km	12 April	Lammers/Watson (Jaguar XJR-8)
Silverstone 1000 km	10 May	Boesel/Cheever (Jaguar XJR-8)
Le Mans 24 hours	13/14 June	Bell/Stuck/Holbert (Porsche 962)
Norisring 360 km	28 June	Baldi/Palmer (Porsche 962)
Brands Hatch 1000 km	26 July	Boesel/Nielsen (Jaguar XJR-8)
Neue N'gring 1000 km	30 Aug	Boesel/Cheever (Jaguar XJR-8)
Spa-F'champs 1000 km*	13 Sept	Boesel/Brundle/Dumfries (XJR-8)
Fuji 1000 km	27 Sept	Lammers/Watson (Jaguar XJR-8)

World Champion: Raul Boesel (Brazilian)
World Champion Team: Silk Cut Jaguar

** Race shortened to 6 hours, due to rain*

Landmarks from 1953

1953 was the first year of the World Sports Car Championship. (Its original format would be retained until 1961, after which there would come a complex mix of sports and GT regulations.)

1958 marked the start of the '3-litre' sports car formula, effectively ruling out Jaguar which had recently withdrawn from racing and did not have a suitable engine anyway.

1959 saw Aston Martin leap to prominence, winning Le Mans for the first and only time and becoming the first British make to win the World Championship which (apart from 1955) continued to be dominated by Ferrari.

1960 marked Porsche's arrival as an overall contender, only just failing to beat Ferrari. Porsche's progress in the 1953 – 1961 World series went as follows: 9th (equal); 6th; 6th; 5th; 5th; 2nd; 3rd; 2nd; 3rd.

1966 saw Ford win Le Mans and the World Championship for the first time. Jaguar considered developing its XJ13 to compete but shelved the idea following the merger with BMC.

1969 was Porsche's first year of overall victory in the championship.

1972 was Ferrari's last year of overall victory in the championship.

1981 saw the introduction of a Drivers' championship.

1984 marked the return of Jaguar to Le Mans, with two US-built Group 44 XJR-5s. They came to Europe the following year (once again, to Le Mans only).

1985 was the first year of the World Championship of Teams as opposed to Makes. The TWR Jaguar team of XJR-6s took part in the last five (of ten) races, and finished the season seventh overall.

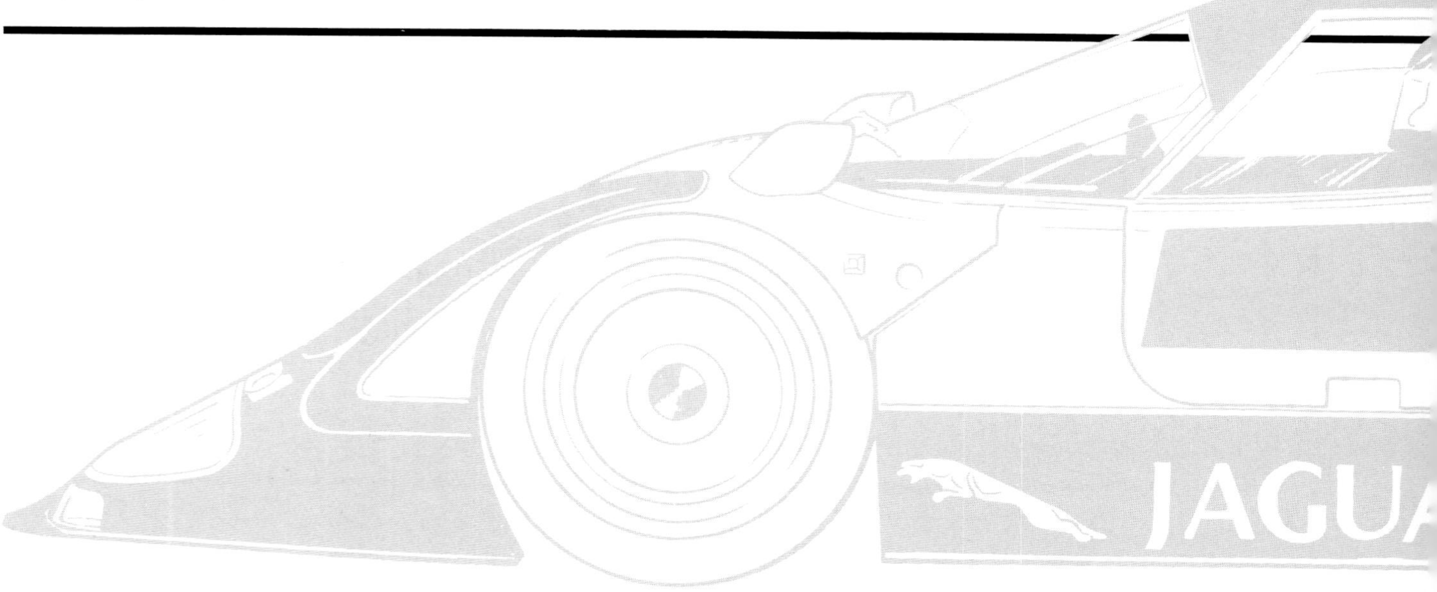

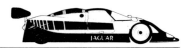

Two Generations of the Championship for marques

	1953 to 1957	
1953	1st	Ferrari
	2nd	***JAGUAR***
	3rd	Aston Martin
	4th	Lancia
1954	1st	Ferrari
	2nd	Lancia
	3rd	***JAGUAR***
	4th	Osca
1955	1st	Mercedes-Benz
	2nd	Ferrari
	3rd	***JAGUAR***
	4th	Maserati
1956	1st	Ferrari
	2nd	Maserati
	3rd	***JAGUAR***
	4th	Aston Martin
1957	1st	Ferrari
	2nd	Maserati
	3rd	***JAGUAR***
	4th	Aston Martin

	1983 to 1987	
1983	1st	Porsche
	2nd	Lancia
	3rd	Nimrod-Aston Martin March-Nissan
1984	1st	Porsche
	2nd	Lancia
	3rd	Rondeau-Cosworth Dome-Toyota
**1985*	1st	Rothmans Porsche
	2nd	Martini Lancia Team
	3rd	Joest Porsche team
	4th	Kremer Porsche team
**1986*	1st	Brun Porsche team
	2nd	Joest Porsche team
	3rd	Rothmans Porsche Silk Cut ***JAGUAR*** team
**1987*	1st	Silk Cut ***JAGUAR*** team
	2nd	Brun Porsche team
	3rd	Rothmans Porsche
	4th	Joest Porsche team

** Makers' championship replaced by Teams' competition from 1985*

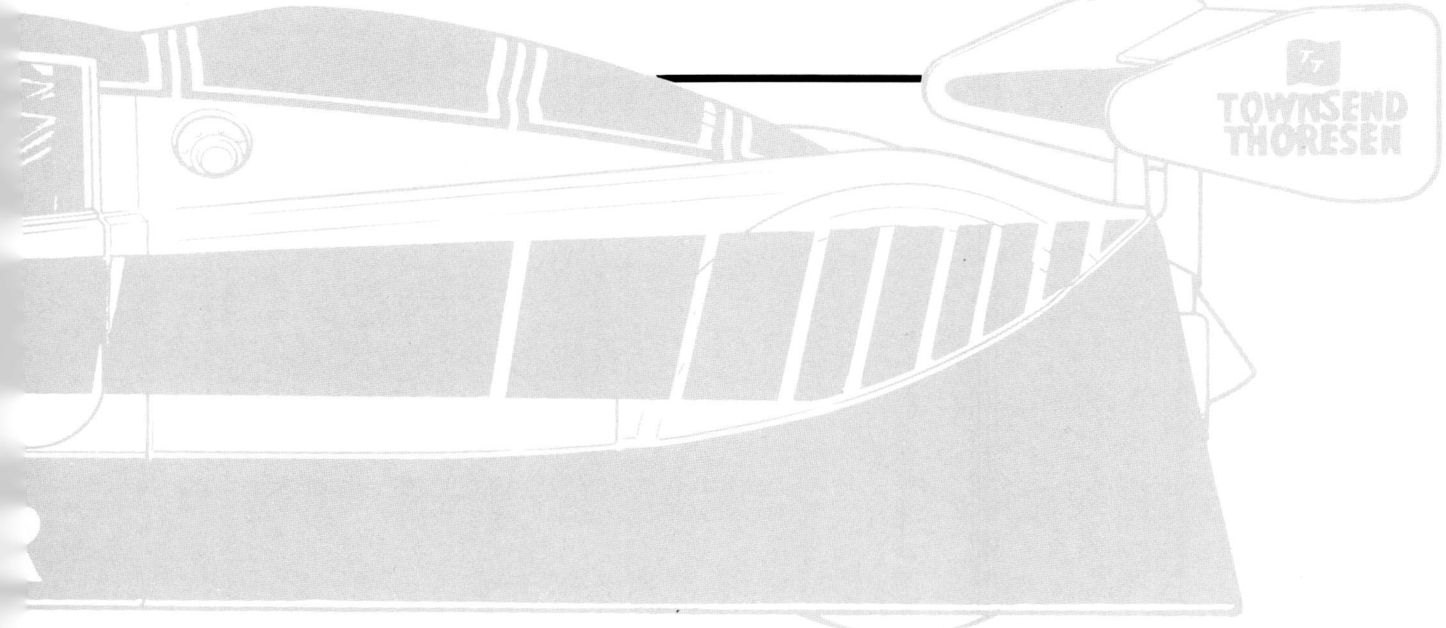

Tom Walkinshaw, *racing driver, at ease in 1984 – the year in which he won the Group A championship of Europe, driving Jaguar XJ-S exclusively. (Tom Walkinshaw, businessman of infinite resolve, chose not to participate in Group C racing himself, despite the natural temptation.) This very nice photograph was taken by Neville Marriner of the* Daily Mail. *In 1988, the Walkinshaw business group's involvement with Jaguar was greater than ever before.*

TWR's first involvement with Jaguar was with the birth of Group A touring car racing in 1982, when Tom Walkinshaw won four ETC races. Sponsored by Motul oil and Akai audio, his XJ-S is seen here at Donington Park prior to that season which was followed by official works backing for 1983.

For its third season with Jaguar, TWR ran three XJ-Ss in the twelve-round European Touring Car Championship. The team won seven races. Formerly dominant, BMW won only four times, and Volvo once. Tom Walkinshaw became European Champion for 1984, when this picture was taken at Vallelunga.

Both the 48-valve engine and the XJR-5 chassis were turned down by TWR in favour of the lighter 24-valve V12 Jaguar power unit in a structure designed by Tony Southgate. Here the brand-new XJR-6 is seen in its livery for 1985 when Castrol replaced Motul as Jaguar's associated oil company in the racing context, although only in a small way initially.

For 1986, Gallaher International came in with major sponsorship, featuring its 'Silk Cut' brand of cigarette. This press-release picture shows (probably accidentally) what the XJR-6 would look like without wheel spats.

Experimental Jaguar 48-valve 'AJ12' engine as fitted to Group 44 XJR-5 IMSA car, and tested by TWR in the winter of 1984-85.

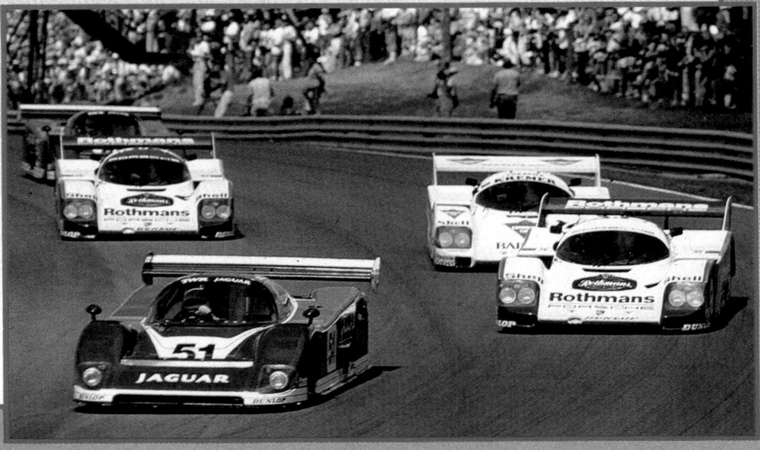

An historic Malcolm Bryan photograph from Mosport, Canada, where the XJR-6 led for several laps of its début event in August 1985. Here the two Jaguars sandwich three Porsche 962s. No.51 was to retire, but No.52 (just visible here) went on to finish third behind the two Rothmans Porsches.

A Good Day: First victory for the XJR-6 was in May 1986, at Silverstone, where it is seen with the man behind the project, Tom Walkinshaw.

The action shot shows the winning Cheever/Warwick car after losing its offside rear wheel spat. 'Silk Cut' lettering was banned at Silverstone in 1986. (Andrew Whyte photos)

Jaguar's chief opposition at Silverstone in 1986 came from the Martini Lancia and Rothmans Porsche teams. Lancia would withdraw from Group C racing but other makes – notably the Mercedes-powered Sauber – were on their way up, to give sports-car racing a truly competitive flavour.

A Bad Day: Potentially, the Silk Cut Jaguar Team had the 1986 Jerez sprint race in its pocket, but an over-eager Derek Warwick turned across the bows of team-mate Gianfranco Brancatelli. Eddie Cheever in a third Jaguar could not avoid the mêlée, so the race (and, as it turned out, the teams' championship) was handed on a plate to the Swiss-entered Porsche team of Walter Brun.

After recovering, Brancatelli (53) and Cheever (51) retired with transmission trouble, caused by the notorious Jerez hump. Warwick (52) lost two laps in the sand and in the pits, but recovered partially to take third place with help from Lammers. (1986 Jerez photos by Malcoln Bryan)

Conditions for the 1986 1000 km race at the *Neue Nürburgring* were atrocious, and it had to be stopped at one point. The Porsches were out of luck that day. Until their XJR-6 broke an oil-pipe, Warwick and Lammers looked like winning. As it was, the impressive black Sauber-Mercedes of Pescarolo and Thackwell – seen here with the Jaguar – scored its first-ever victory. (Malcolm Bryan photos)

3

JAGUAR & TWR

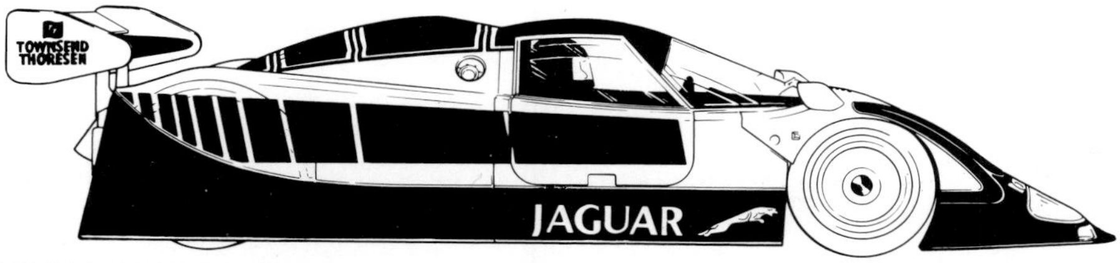

Jaguar, Racing and Sponsorship

In its early motor racing history Jaguar Cars Limited followed the trend of the times. It built and developed and raced its own cars; or it sold or lent cars, with or without providing subsequent service, to private teams or individuals. Jaguar made its own contracts with the drivers, among whom only the team leaders – first Stirling Moss, then Mike Hawthorn – were full-time race drivers. There were some funds and success bonuses from the suppliers of components, but there was no racing budget. The racing was incidental to Jaguar's main business – that of car-making. As Raymond ('Lofty') England, the former racing manager of Jaguar, wrote in his foreword to my two-volume history of the marque in competitions: "For the management and staff involved, the competition work was just an addition to their normal responsibilities and not to be taken as an excuse for something else not getting done – as witness what was achieved by Chief Engineer Bill Heynes and his handful of engineers who in the ten immediate postwar years, in addition to designing and producing the C-type and the D-type competition cars, designed and got into production four completely new Jaguars *and* many variations of them."

Times have changed, but one aspect of racing has stayed the same since Jaguar's return to prosperity under Sir John Egan's leadership: the need to win what you set out to win, whether it is a particular championship or one of the great marathons like the 24 hours of Le Mans or Francorchamps, or that giant television promotion for which all Australia stops once a year, the 1000 km of Bathurst.

In earlier times there were fewer races and the media possibilities were more basic. The whole game – even including Formula One Grand Prix racing – was contained within comprehensible financial limits.

The XJR-8 in its 1987 livery, with space priority going to the product of the main sponsor, Gallaher International. Also prominent are the names of Castrol (who have been with the Jaguar Group C project from the start, in 1985), Dunlop, Townsend Thoresen, and TWR itself.

Thirty-five years earlier, advertising was the exception rather than the rule. This XK120, with Disney-like caricatures on the front wings, completed the 1952 **Carrera Panamericana** *Mexico driven by Douglas Ehlinger, who dedicated the photograph to Jaguar's competitions manager of the time, Mort Morris-Goodall.*

Sometimes cars must race without the sponsor's wording, as when the XJR-6 gained its first-ever victory (at Silverstone) in 1986; but when the colours are familiar or striking, the absence of a product name is hardly noticed.

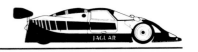

In Jaguar's early racing days, there was no sponsorship and no racing budget. Editorial coverage and a little advertising were sufficient reward, for there were few races to compete for editorial space. With a plain, unadorned paint job, nothing distracted the eye away from the beauty of the vehicle. This famous works Jaguar XK120 is seen being driven by Peter Whitehead in the 1950 Tourist Trophy race at Dundrod, Northern Ireland.

The Jaguar XK120C won its first motor race, the 1951 24 hours of Le Mans – something no manufacturer could expect to do now. Afterwards, it was put on display in the Piccadilly showroom of Henlys, the main Jaguar UK distributor. Nowadays, there would be a dummy car for showroom use, or a large scale model. Race cars were required to work just as **hard** *when they were racing in those days, but not nearly as* **often** *as their modern counterparts.*

Nowadays, the cost of a slice of the action is measured in multiples of millions. No manufacturer can go motor racing without a budget; and to find an adequate budget entirely within his own resources would do nothing to woo his shareholders. Jaguar has been back in the shares business since the summer of 1984, when the Jaguar Group A European project was about to 'wind down' as Tom Walkinshaw was being hailed the European Champion and already seeking new conquests. The change of direction was towards Group C sports-cars. Secretly, the XJR-6 was already well under way when Jaguar began to make its own moves to find a major sponsor in early 1985. Jaguar's then sales and marketing supremo, Neil Johnson, and Nigel Heslop (at that time Staff Director, Product and Business Strategy) began exploring the unfamiliar field of sponsorship. They did not have the experience nor the time to go deal-hunting alone. With the help of Castrol and Townsend Thorensen, there were sufficient funds to make a commitment to proceed with a part-season in 1985, assuming the XJR-6 showed the right potential – that meant the potential to beat Porsche. A further three-year contract – the minimum reasonable period from most viewpoints – was not forthcoming so far. Outside expertise was needed (it was agreed at a Jaguar Board meeting). This all coincided with a press article on the Edwards system. In March 1985, Guy Edwards received his first phone call from Jaguar.

Most people thought the D-type's curves spoke for themselves; but the D-type **was** *a production car – albeit a limited edition – and needed selling in 1955 and 1956, North America being the best market potentially. (In fact, it proved very difficult to sell, and several D-types were modified into XKSSs in 1957 to* **appear** *more like road cars.)*

What's in a name? In 1977, when Jaguar came under BL rule, Leyland decided to go racing with the XJ12 two-door model as a highly modified Group 2 car. The spectacular cars were prepared for the ETC series by Broadspeed, and they led every race at some stage – but they never won. Jaguar's own engineers had not approved the plan, and were not surprised. On one occasion, at the Nürburgring, all but one of the BMW CSLs ran into trouble, and one of the Broadspeed cars came second. That was one of only two finishes all told for the 'Big Cats', as the BL Motorsport organisation dubbed then. 'Leyland' may have been the promotion, but the cars **looked** *like Jaguars.*

Edwards is still something of a racing folk-hero. It was he who did so much on the spur of the moment in the 1976 German Grand Prix to save the life of Niki Lauda. Edwards had raced until July 1984 when, during a Porsche drive in the 1000 km race at Brands Hatch, he made up his mind that he had had enough. He had had a pretty good innings for someone who knew he would never reach the highest echelon of drivers; often, he had arranged his own sponsorship. He had developed a taste for the promotions business, and was involved in the March team and in Suzuki racing motor cycles. He was also close to Rothmans, the tobacco giant without whose long-term support Porsche might not have stayed in endurance racing as a works team – and that, of course, *could* have meant no world-class sports-car racing at all. (As it was, Porsche was so dominant that the manufacturers' title was replaced in 1985 by a teams' championship. This oiled wheels by providing further opportunities to mention sponsors' names.)

Edwards got to work on his shortlist of over twenty major companies which his instinct and experience told him *might* be interested. He told me: "I was given a free hand to go hunting. The only limitations were that we must keep within the bounds of good taste, and to treat strong liquor as a no-go area." Among those companies which Edwards feels came quite near to a Jaguar deal was American Express. In fact, British Caledonian came *very* close; but, as with Porsche and other leading racing teams, it was a tobacco group that was won over.

Edwards had, in fact, rescinded his vow not to race again. He drove a Fitzpatrick Porsche 956 at Le Mans in 1985 with David Hobbs and Jo Gartner; they came fourth. *That* drive was related to a tie-up with a special Gallaher brand name: American 100s. Peter Gilpin had just moved (as Chairman) to Gallaher International from Rothmans and was, apparently, keen to have Le Mans on his programme.

"It's all to do with winning," said Edwards, at the end of the 1987

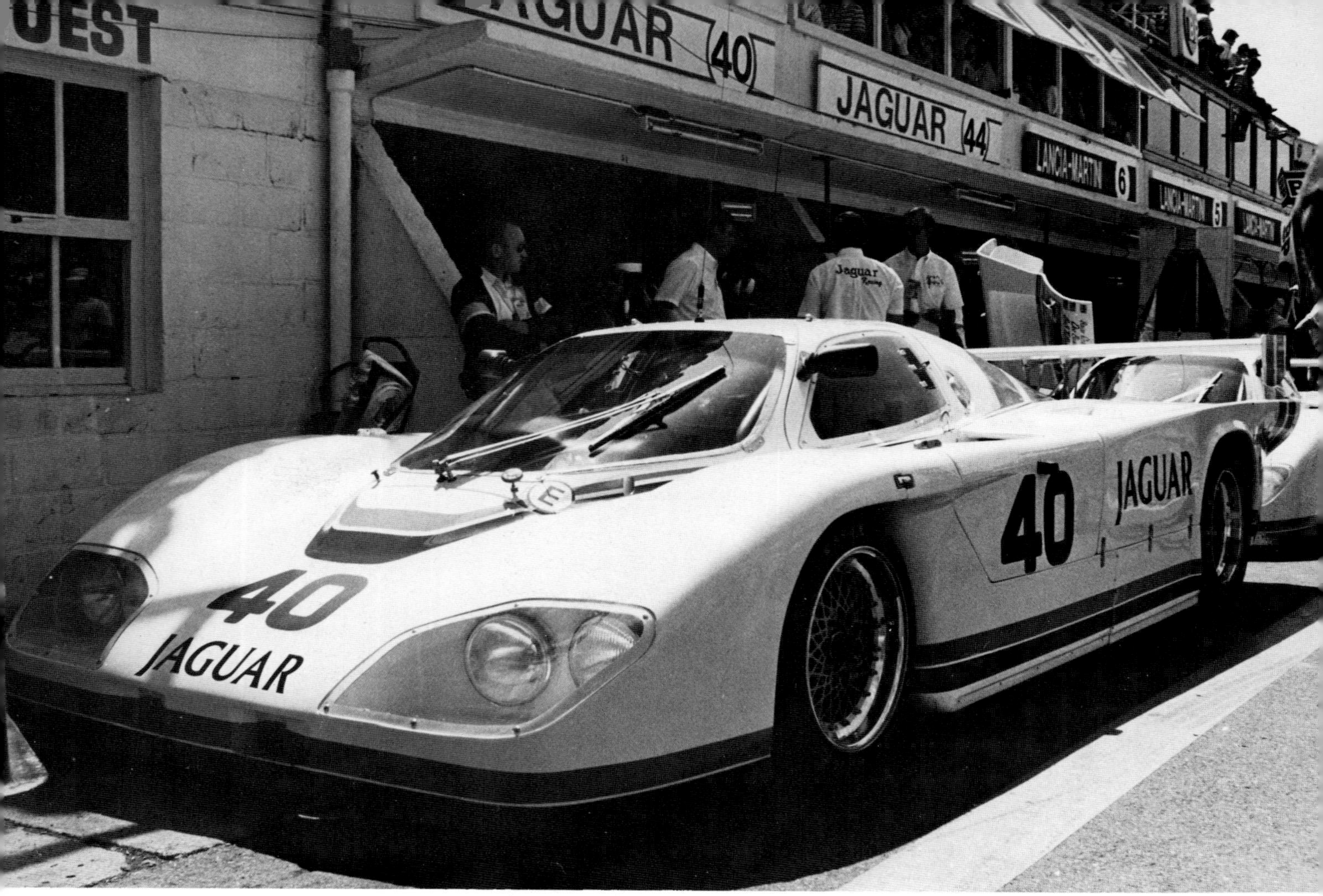

By contrast, the later American designed and built XJR-5 was not a Jaguar in the true sense – yet it carried the name proudly. And why not? – for the power unit (like those of the other 'XJR' mid-engined race cars) was a modified version of the Coventry's famous V12. It did not look *like a Jaguar, but was very distinctive in its own right – and in 1984 it brought the marque name back to Le Mans for the first time in twenty years.*

The Business: *Even after Jaguar adopted Tom Walkinshaw's successful Group A programme officially, the 'TWR' emblem remained. Tom Walkinshaw Racing Ltd had become a very big business in many different* fields, and its fame has continued to spread. This shot was also taken at the Old Nürburgring during the last international long-distance race to be held there, in 1983. (Walkinshaw and 'Nicholson' had won with an XJ-S the previous year but failed to finish on this occasion.)

In early 1984, 'TWR Jaguar Sport' came into being with a range of cosmetic and internal modifications for the roadgoing XJ-S, and it had its own Brussels Show stand.

season. Awareness of the Silk Cut brand name since the Jaguar deal went through has more than doubled. In any case, someone decided that the Silk Cut cigarette had 'feminine' overtones. Gallaher wanted it to become more of a man's cigarette, and the name of Jaguar plus the aggressive nature of racing appealed to Gilpin.

Jaguar and Gallaher signed their deal in September 1985. TWR, although assumed to be racing with Jaguars, did not complete their three-year agreement until later in the year. Maybe Tom Walkinshaw was just making sure of his place in the equation.

There was not too much bad publicity when details of the new Silk Cut Jaguar Team were announced from Coventry on 14 January 1986, although Coventry's own newspaper, the *Evening Telegraph* carried an editorial criticising Jaguar for its Gallaher tie up: *In painting their cars purple and white and displaying the words 'Silk Cut' whenever possible, Jaguar may be giving their shareholders a good deal. But the cost will undoubtedly be paid later by some of those whose custom Gallaher are hoping to attract through their investment.*

On an inside page, motoring correspondent Keith Read quoted David Simpson (director of the anti-smoking group ASH) as deploring Jaguar's decision. Jaguar's racing press relations man Ian Norris was quick to respond. "One is aware of the feeling against smoking," he told Read. "We were looking for a sponsor who could match our aims in racing . . . the Formula One World Championship has been won by a tobacco company – McLaren with Marlboro – and tobacco sponsorship in motor sport is an accepted fact."

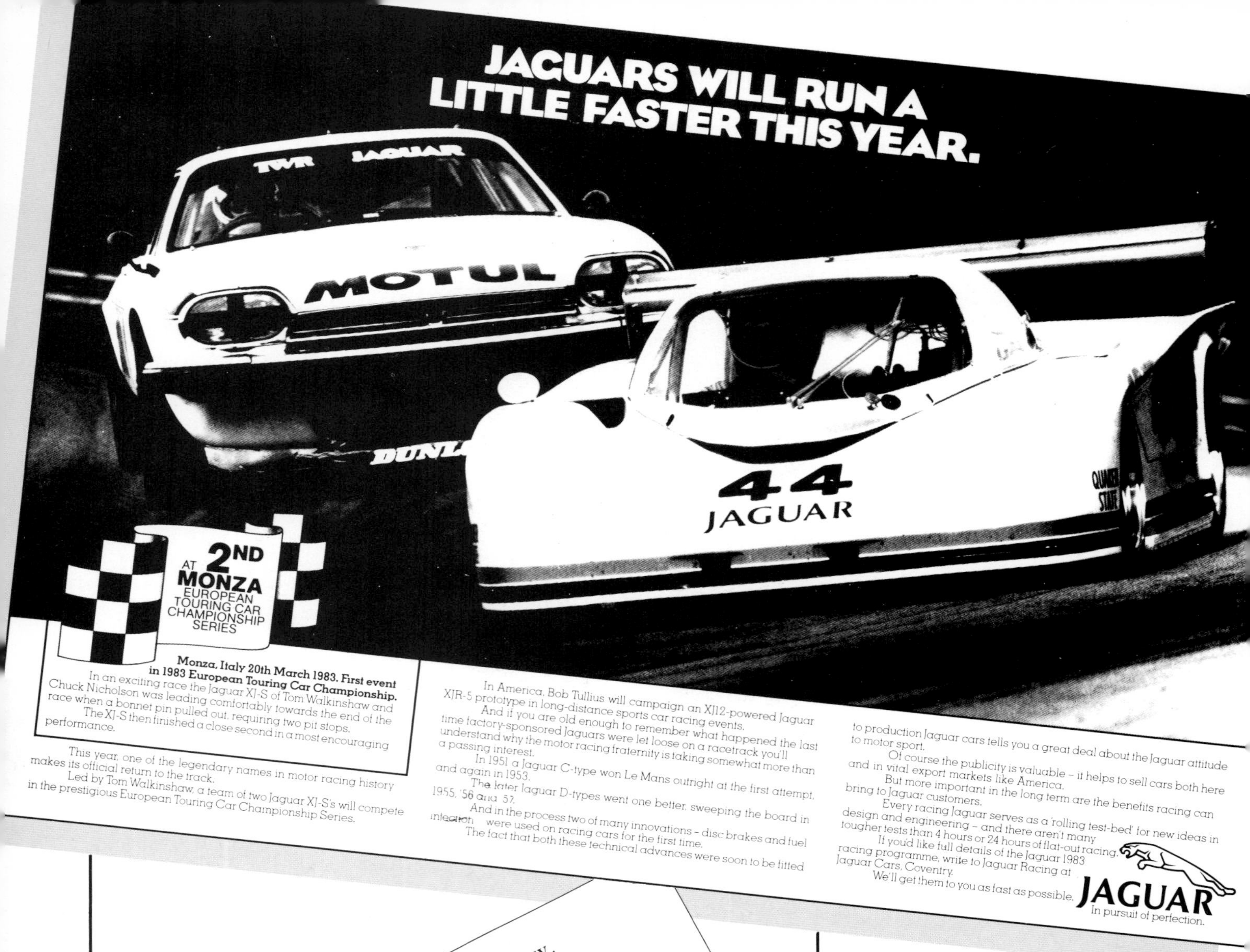
JAGUARS WILL RUN A LITTLE FASTER THIS YEAR.
AT 2ND MONZA EUROPEAN TOURING CAR CHAMPIONSHIP SERIES
Monza, Italy 20th March 1983. First event in 1983 European Touring Car Championship.
In an exciting race the Jaguar XJ-S of Tom Walkinshaw and Chuck Nicholson was leading comfortably towards the end of the race when a bonnet pin pulled out, requiring two pit stops.
The XJ-S then finished a close second in a most encouraging performance.
This year, one of the legendary names in motor racing history makes its official return to the track.
Led by Tom Walkinshaw, a team of two Jaguar XJ-S's will compete in the prestigious European Touring Car Championship Series.
In America, Bob Tullius will campaign an XJ12-powered Jaguar XJR-5 prototype in long-distance sports car racing events.
And if you are old enough to remember what happened the last time factory-sponsored Jaguars were let loose on a racetrack you'll understand why the motor racing fraternity is taking somewhat more than a passing interest.
In 1951 a Jaguar C-type won Le Mans outright at the first attempt, and again in 1953.
The later Jaguar D-types went one better, sweeping the board in 1955, '56 and '57.
And in the process two of many innovations – disc brakes and fuel injection – were used on racing cars for the first time.
The fact that both these technical advances were soon to be fitted to production Jaguar cars tells you a great deal about the Jaguar attitude to motor sport.
Of course the publicity is valuable – it helps to sell cars both here and in vital export markets like America.
But more important in the long term are the benefits racing can bring to Jaguar customers.
Every racing Jaguar serves as a 'rolling test-bed' for new ideas in design and engineering – and there aren't many tougher tests than 4 hours or 24 hours of flat-out racing.
If you'd like full details of the Jaguar 1983 racing programme, write to Jaguar Racing at Jaguar Cars, Coventry.
We'll get them to you as fast as possible.
JAGUAR
In pursuit of perfection.

SILVERSTONE. FOUR IN A ROW.
XJR8
JAGUAR RACING
JAGUAR

Advertising: A change of emphasis.

Jaguar's reappearance on the racing scene in March 1983 had been as long-awaited by the enthusiast as the company's self-determination by the potential customer. "This year [read the advertising copy] one of the legendary names in motor racing history makes its official return to the track. Led by Tom Walkinshaw, a team of two XJ-Ss will compete in the prestigious European Touring Car Championship series. In America Bob Tullius will campaign an XJ12-powered Jaguar XJR-5 prototype in long-distance sports car racing events." The advertisement recalled past Le Mans successes and explained that the comeback was not just a publicity stunt: "Every racing Jaguar serves as a 'rolling test-bed' for new ideas in design and engineering . . Four years later, when it had been decided not to develop the XJ-S further for touring car racing, there was a distinct change of emphasis, for there was no relationship between the new generation of Group C cars and any roadgoing Jaguar other than in the basic V12 engine components. By 1987, Jaguar's sales and marketing function was, more than ever, the controlling force in the racing programme, and the advertising now went no further than to say: "Our continued spirit of success on the track is reflected in every Jaguar we build for the road." In other words: We all like to be associated with a winning name. Note how the SILK CUT lettering has been retouched out of the picture.

Advertising standards and Jaguar's own views made sure that the product (*not* the sponsor's product) and racing got promoted through direct publicity. John Egan, not a cigarette smoker himself, kept out of the sponsorship discussion: "Racing is an integral part of Jaguar's heritage," he said. "We know the competition will be fierce, but we have learned to respect Tom Walkinshaw and his team at TWR and we know that with their wholehearted professionalism allied to our own technical back-up, we can expect the best from our cars on the track."

Within two years, the prophesies had come true. The only policy change, once Jaguar was settled into Group C rather than Group A, was a reduction of technical exchange with Coventry. This was emphasised later on, when racing liaison manager Ron Elkins was transferred from Engineering to Sales and Marketing. Elkins' assistant, Peter Dodd, however – who had been at Jaguar long enough to remember the Company's last in-house racing projects – remained with Jim Randle's Engineering Department as it moved from Browns Lane to its new £50 million HQ at Whitley on the other side of Coventry. Here Jaguar's rig facilities could be of great use to TWR, through Dodd's assistance.

Jaguar-engined powerboats have been around for many years, and the large external surface area makes good advertising space. Vodka-sponsored **Vladivar** *was a mid-seventies reincarnation of the late Norman Buckley's* **Miss Windermere V.** *Buckley's protégé Tony Fahey took several international records with this craft, which had a V12 engine prepared by Forward Engineering with some assistance from BL/Jaguar.*

In order to move quickly and adapt to trends, a small specialised department is required – dedicated to the task of winning. As Group C racing cars bore little or no resemblance to road cars, there were few, if any, areas in which Jaguar could use experience with the former to improve the latter. Motor racing is a totally commercial activity, based on the need to generate business.

To its many recent accolades, Jaguar can now add the title: World Champion. The only way it could improve on that would be to win again at Le Mans, where Jaguar acquired its racing heritage.

In the 1980s, two offshore powerboats were sponsored by Jaguar and Peter Stuyvesant. One of them – **Goldrush,** *seen here – was late re-named* **The Legend** *(also shown) to fit in with Jaguar's marketing slogan 'The Legend Grows'. But the boat itself was not a Jaguar despite its twin turbocharged*

V12 engines, and it became apparent that the name meant so much more when applied to a motor car – even if the car was not a Coventry product. Once the Group C project was off the ground in 1985, Jaguar became less interested in water sports.

Jaguar and Castrol: *Castrol (formerly Wakefield, then Burmah) has been associated with motor sports for many a long year. Traditionally, the Jaguar works team was contracted to use Shell products, while* **Ecurie Ecosse** *had been with Esso ever since that company had given the independent Scottish Jaguar team £1000 to get it started in 1952. In 1963 Castrol instigated a joint exercise at Monza, where a works-prepared 3.8-litre Mark 2 saloon took several long-distance speed records. It was driven by Geoff Duke as team leader plus John Bekaert, Andrew Hedges, Peter Lumsden and Peter Sargent, all of whom are in this picture taken by the author just before the start. Also visible are Jaguar's 'Lofty' England* **(extreme left)** and Castrol's Jimmy Hill **(under 'Z' of Monza).**

At the wheel of the Castrol Jaguar 3.8 in the banking shot is John Bekaert, one of Britain's best club drivers of the day (Monza, 1963).

When Jaguar and TWR decided to go in for Group C sports-prototype racing in 1985 (prior to the 'Silk Cut' deal), it was Castrol who came up with some backing for the TWR XJR-6, seen here on test at Donington Park shortly before being shipped to Canada for its first race. It wore its dark green and white livery for that half-season, before reappearing for 1986 in more garish guise. The Castrol involvement has continued, however, and 1988 saw not only the continuation of 'Silk Cut' brand for a third season of Group C, but the arrival of a new Castrol-sponsored TWR-Jaguar assault on the North American 'GT-prototype' racing scene.

The Transport: *Cars have to be transported to motor races, although it was not always so. The picture of the Mark Seven and the works C-type was taken en route to the 1952 Mille Miglia. Works cars were*

always driven on the road. The Jaguar company never used a race-car transporter – ever! – but it did, of course, have to send the odd Bedford lorry or van-load of parts to races.

Ecurie Ecosse *had a Bedford box van in their early days, too, plus a succession of equally elderly buses or coaches, converted to carry cars – and suppliers' advertising!*

TWR's articulated transporter is typical of the professional team's equipment today. It is seen in Austria in 1984, when the Group A Jaguars were

dominant. It is noteworthy that Motul, the team's original sponsor, was virtually out of the picture by then. Repainted for Jaguar's Group C era (in the purple, gold and white of 'Silk Cut') the transporter clearly shows Castrol allegiance at Spa.

The Gear: In the old days, drivers tended to wear any old thing, and were recognisable by their features, their driving style and their apparel – all of which were easy to see. 'B. Bira', who drove the XK120 in its first race at Silverstone in 1949, cut a dapper figure but, like many others, eschewed a crash helmet. Swashbuckling Duncan Hamilton raced in shirt-sleeves and sometimes a pullover but at least he decided to acquire some head protection – as more and more people began to do from the early 1950s.

Mike Hawthorn and his predecessor as Jaguar team leader, Stirling Moss, combined individualism with practicality. In or out of a car, you could not fail to recognise either.

The modern racing driver is just as individual, but his protective garb renders him virtually anonymous – although a personal helmet pattern helps identification. 1986 Silk Cut Jaguar Team driver Jean-Louis Schlesser advertises the right things in the right proportions. (1987 drivers had the Townsend

Thoresen insignia on their overalls, too.) Actually, you can learn a lot about people and places from the detail differences. The helmet says this is Eddie Cheever and the lack of the words 'Silk Cut' suggests Germany. This is, in fact, the winning car of Cheever/Boesel in the **Neue Nürburgring** *1000 km race, from which the team emerged as the 1987 World Champions. After the race, of course, you can tell who everyone is, despite the shadow cast by further commercial headgear. Here Lammers, Nielsen, Boesel and Watson share the glory after their one-three finish at Brands Hatch in 1987.*

Silk Cut Jaguar, exhibited at the Amsterdam Show in February 1987, when the Tony Southgate-designed car had just received a British Design Council Award. Shortly afterwards, the model name was changed from XJR-6 to XJR-8.

The Tom Walkinshaw Influence

Between 1981 and 1987, Tom Walkinshaw Racing Ltd (TWR) orchestrated the return of Jaguar to the highest pinnacle of sports car racing. It was, in a sense, a repeat of the first meteoric performance in motor sports, thirty years earlier.

From 1951 to 1957, Jaguar Cars Ltd operated its own effective competitions programme and the name Jaguar became something special in world terms as the original company was growing up. Le Mans was won five times, and there were victories for works cars at other great circuits, from Reims to Sebring, and in classic road events such as the *Marathon de la Route* and the Monte Carlo Rally.

After it withdrew from competitions – until it became part of British Motor Holdings, and then British Leyland – Jaguar continued to develop ideas and assist successful private teams and individuals.

Introduction of the XJ6 in 1968 led to a change of image for Jaguar, and racing did not seem so appropriate – although, during the brief XJ12 'Broadspeed' era, BL thought otherwise. Only when the XJ-S came on the scene did it seem possible that the marque might re-emerge in international racing. Indeed, Bob Tullius and Group 44 had rekindled the flame effectively in the USA, where the national regulations fitted around the V12 E-type and XJ-S well enough to make them winners in SCCA events.

In Europe, however, there was no opportunity to make the XJ-S a race winner at the right level – although Jaguar engineers did undertake tentative projects to assess their own capabilities against those of the potential opposition. The company no longer possessed its independence in the late nineteen-seventies, and only the strong will and sheer bloody-mindedness of technical director Robert Knight saved Jaguar from the loss of individuality that has befallen every other BL marque.

As the new decade began, Jaguar production was at an all-time economic low; then came new hope, in the form of John Egan. He arrived at Jaguar in April 1980; but it was going to take many more months to establish whether Jaguar would be allowed to survive at all. Nothing could have been further from Egan's mind than motor racing.

By contrast, at an industrial estate beside the Kidlington aerodrome, just north of Oxford, the business portents seemed promising. Tom Walkinshaw had encountered failure and success – good times and bad times, good teams and bad teams – ever since he had begun racing as a hobby in 1966. He had turned it into a business, gaining experience quickly by developing a close association with Ford and BMW. From 1978 his business, TWR, had occupied its own premises at Kidlington, and Walkinshaw had widened his interests to embrace Mazda and BL racing projects as well as other work involving the motor industry and trade.

Whereas Jaguar had lost touch with motor racing while it struggled to make a road car to a quality worthy of the basic design, TWR was fast-moving and adaptable. It could change course quickly to take advantage of situations and opportunities as they presented themselves.

The opportunity of 1981 was the announcement of full details of a new-for-'82 international touring car race formula: Group A.

Group A touring cars had to *look* like their roadgoing counterparts, and their engine modifications were to be restricted. There was, however, considerable scope for making transmission and braking systems cope with a typical 500 km, ETC race. The inaugural European Touring Car racing championship in 1963 had been won by Peter Nöcker of West Germany, driving works-prepared Jaguar 3.8-litre saloons entered and maintained by the German importer, Peter Lindner. More recently Tom Walkinshaw had seen, and contributed to, the BMW domination of ETC racing. He wanted to be champion himself and, with Group A, he saw a way of achieving this personal aim in a British car.

In 1981, Walkinshaw convinced Jaguar's new management team – in particular John Egan and the technical chief (Knight's successor) James Randle – that their XJ-S was not only eligible for Group A, but that it could win. His ambition was boundless, but he was not too disappointed when he was told he would have to race unofficially . . . to start with, anyway.

In my book *Jaguar Sports Racing and Works Competition Cars from 1954,* chapters Fifteen and Sixteen cover the TWR-Jaguar story in some detail – up to the start of its brilliant sixth full season: 1987.

The following pages are intended as a background to what has been achieved, and to provide an introduction to the story of a magic season.

Initially, Jaguar provided TWR with technical and material assistance, but the Group A project would succeed or fail as a Kidlington exercise, *not* a Coventry one. Press rumours and counter-rumours prevailed in the winter of 1981/82. In March 1982, TWR made its own announcement of the formation of Team Motul Jaguar.

Team
MOTUL
JAGUAR

For the first few races, the smart black coupé (sponsored by the French oil company) had teething troubles, although Walkinshaw did win a minor race in Belgium in the spring. In June 1982, the small team run by Paul Davis ***(seen here at Brno)*** was getting to grips with the problems.

With 'Chuck Nicholson' co-driving, Walkinshaw gave the XJ-S its first ETC race win on the fast, hilly Brno road circuit which suited it so well. (Walkinshaw would win here for Jaguar in 1983 and 1984, too.)

After Brno there was a more significant victory at the Nürburgring, although little was made of it at the time. In the latter part of the season, a second car joined the team. One-Two results were posted at Silverstone and Zolder, to give Walkinshaw and 'Nicholson' four wins and to place them third and fourth (to the Kelleners/Grano BMW combination) in the 1982 European championship. This is the Dieudonné/Lovett car which was runner-up in the TT at Silverstone.

For 1983, Jaguar stood behind TWR officially; although the Motul contract was continued. Here are Tom Walkinshaw and the white-and-green car at the official launch in London.

For 1983, the major BMW teams fielded the newly-homologated 635CSi (instead of the 528i) and they made the two-car TWR Jaguar team work very hard all season. This picture was taken during the opening round at Monza.

Jaguar's John Egan, Jim Randle, and sales and marketing director Neil Johnson had cause to look serious at Monza, where trouble with a Jaguar bonnet pin gave BMW's Dieter Quester the race – and, as it would turn out, the championship. (There were to be irritating problems at the next two races, too, although Round Three did go to Jaguar, thanks to the scintillating wet weather driving of Martin Brundle.)

Tom Walkinshaw's 1983 wins began at Pergusa near Enna in central Sicily.

TWR JAGUAR
16
MOTUL
ETERNA-UHREN
23
DUNLOP
DUNLOP

'Nicholson' and Walkinshaw on the rostrum at Pergusa, 1983.

By the middle of 1983, the two TWR Motul Jaguars were dominating the field on the fast circuits of Central Europe, and Walkinshaw led the championship comfortably. Here, at Zeltweg, the XJ-Ss of Walkinshaw/'Nicholson' (1st) and Dieudonné/Calderari (2nd) set off, flanking the Schnitzer-Eterna BMW of Hans-Joachim Stuck and Walter Brun which came third. Later in the season however, the BMWs would become dominant again and, in the very last race, Quester would take the championship from under Walkinshaw's nose.

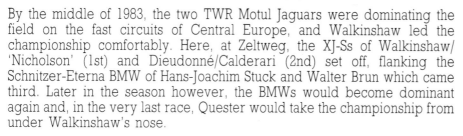

1984: TWR Jaguars won seven of the year's first nine ETC races, while Walkinshaw and his new co-driver, former champion Hans Heyer, built up a substantial lead in the drivers' table. Unfortunately, the marking system was such that it would have been well nigh impossible for any outright race winner to take the manufacturers' title. Alfa Romeo, with virtually no opposition in their class, *had* to be champions. Walkinshaw and Heyer ***(seen here)*** would take first and second places in the drivers' championship, however.

There were many reasons for BMW's continued success, one of which was, simply, force of numbers. 1984 promised to be more competitive, with Rovers and turbo-charged Volvos taking the series more seriously. The regular Jaguar team strength was increased to three cars. Ironically, Walkinshaw was able to obtain a contract to race a Rover Vitesse team in Europe, despite being committed to win for Jaguar! Here all four makes charge through the first Monza chicane together.

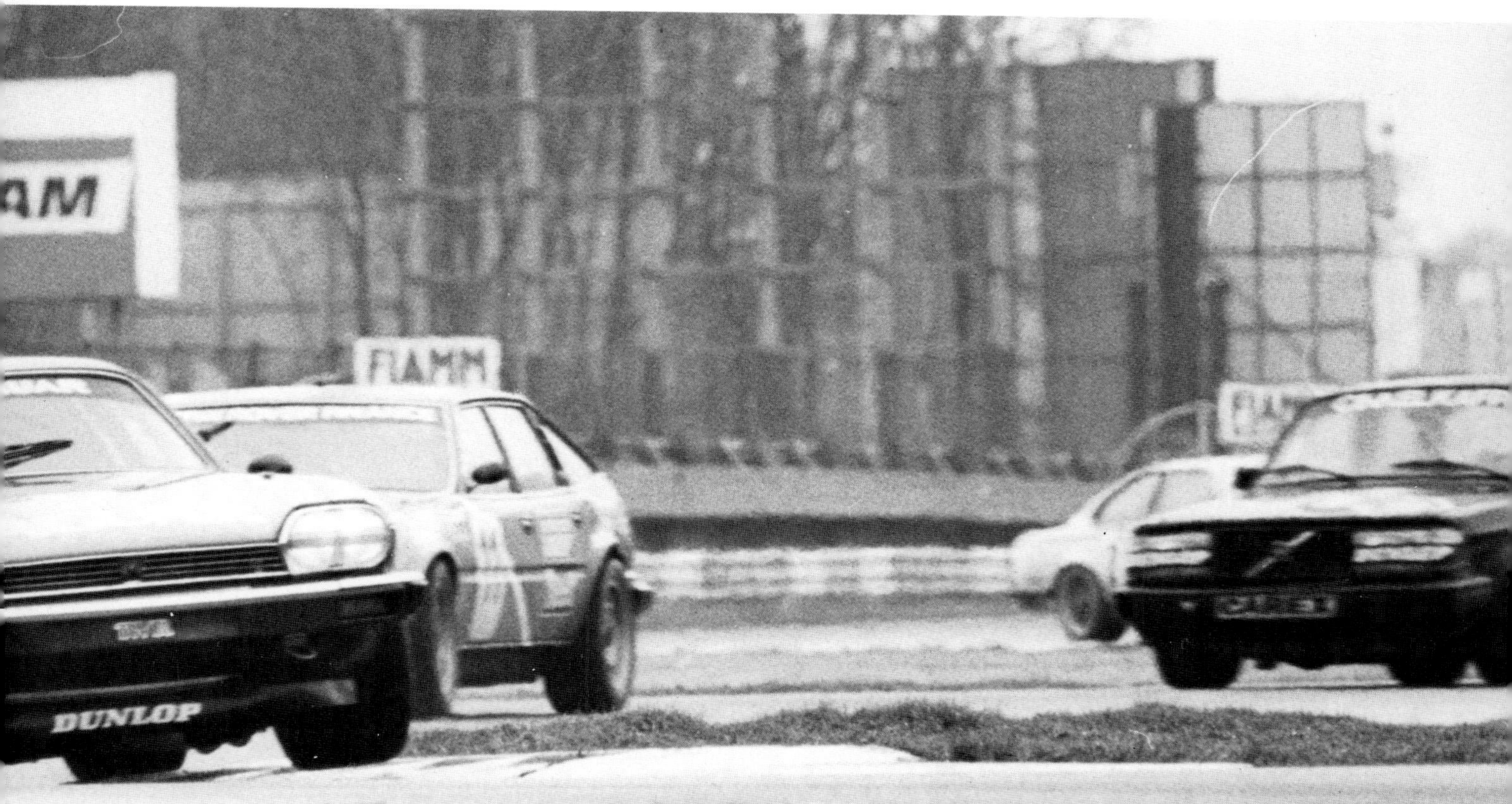

Just as important as the team chief's personal success was the Jaguar victory at Francorchamps. This 24-hour race is the touring car equivalent to Le Mans, and 1984 was the third attempt for the XJ-S. On this occasion, Win Percy shared the honours with Walkinshaw and Heyer. The jewel in the crown was the win at Bathurst. This was duly achieved in 1985, to give the TWR Jaguar its twentieth Group A victory.

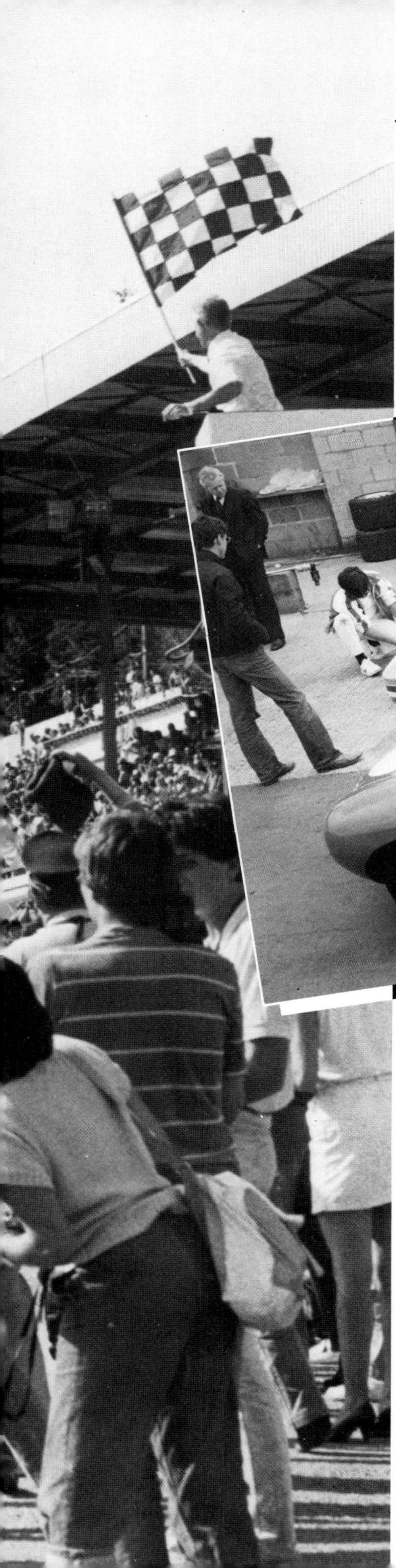

While TWR was reaching the pinnacle of touring car racing, Group 44 had begun racing its mid-engined IMSA GTP car, the V12 Jaguar-powered XJR-5. This American-built car was brought to Silverstone in mid 1983, and tested (with Porsche's approval) by none other than Derek Bell. As a result, Group 44 was appointed to represent Jaguar at Le Mans in 1984.

Not everyone saw the logic of having two Jaguar race teams. Soon after Le Mans 1984 Tom Walkinshaw was talking to Tony Southgate about a new sports car. Southgate ***(seen here)*** had a fine 'track record' as a designer – not only of Formula One cars, but sports/GT prototypes, too. He played a part in creating that important milestone, the 1963 Lola GT (which inspired Jaguar's own stillborn XJ13) and his modern freelance design work is particularly evident in the Group B Ford RS200.

While Southgate worked in secret on a Group C design, TWR obtained an American XJR-5 (ex-Birmingham motor show, 1984) with Jaguar's help, and fitted it with what might be called an 'AJ12' power unit: that is to say, an experimental 48-valve Jaguar V12 engine. The car was painted in TWR's then-current dark green and white livery, and track-tested in early 1985 at Donington Park and Silverstone, where this picture was taken by *Autosport's* Jeff Bloxham. At the time, both Group 44 and TWR had potential Le Mans entries. The power unit was shelved, as it showed no advantage at the time, and the car was returned to Group 44 livery as a museum piece, for Jaguar's own historic collection. But the seeds were now sown for TWR's début in a new arena.

1985 saw Group 44's XJR-5 make its second bid at Le Mans and, although Bob Tullius did finish, it was a troubled run. Moreover, Group 44 was having difficulty in producing victories at home. TWR did not take up its Le Mans option. Instead, the Southgate project was going ahead at full speed. By this time, Jaguar had decided to back the Southgate design all the way. That meant finding a major sponsor. The man who held the Jaguar racing purse-strings was sales and marketing director, Neil Johnson ***(seen above right)***, who would leave Jaguar for a full-time military career in 1986.

Together with his colleague Nigel Heslop, Johnson decided to approach a proved promotions man, Guy Edwards ***(seen opposite left)***, to get the best possible deal.

While Guy Edwards was still negotiating hard, the first Southgate car was nearing completion. A quiet arrival at TWR early in 1984 had been Roger Silman – a local man with many years' experience of race-car fabrication, preparation, and management. Walkinshaw's ability to pick a winner was never demonstrated better than by Silman during the 1987 season. He is shown ***(centre right)*** with Southgate at Donington just two years earlier. In the other picture Silman and Walkinshaw are seen at the *Neue Nürburgring* in 1984, when Walkinshaw was on the point of achieving his personal driving ambition – to become European touring car champion. Publicly, at least, there was never any suggestion that the Scot would drive a Group C car.

DAILY EXPRESS
KROOKLOK
KROOKLO
JAGUAR
51
H64

July 1985 saw first serious testing of the Southgate car, which carried Castrol insiginia from the start. On the right Kevin Lee, Paul Davis, and Rod Benoist confer.

The Southgate car, soon to be introduced as the XJR-6 (to Bob Tullius's chagrin) is seen in action at Donington, July 1985, driven by Mike Thackwell.

Handling problems persisted during July 1985 testing at Donington, with Brundle and Thackwell driving. A planned first appearance at Hockenheim on 14 July was therefore dropped at short notice.

On 11 August 1985, the TWR-built XJR-6 made its spectacular début at Mosport, Canada, with Martin Brundle swooping past Ickx and Stuck (Porsches) to take the lead. Jaguar No.51 was to retire with wheel bearing failure, but the other car (No.52) went on to take third place, driven by Schlesser and Thackwell with assistance from Brundle.

Jaguar was conducting its own sponsorship arrangements with Guy Edwards as the intermediary. Final negotiations took place on 12 September, and on 20 September the main Group C sponsorship deal was signed. On the following day, at Brands Hatch, both XJR-6s retired – but that was just a hiccup, which is part of racing *un*certainty. Seen here are the top men of Jaguar and Gallaher International: John Egan and Peter Gilpin.

The dark green XJR-6s made their fifth and final 1985 appearance at Selangor in December, taking a satisfying second place which put TWR seventh in the Group C team championship despite competing in only half of all WEC events. By this time, TWR had fitted itself into the financial equation and on 14 January 1986 the Silk Cut sponsorship deal was made public. This was the first official photograph to be issued.

1986 was to prove a season of mixed fortunes, a little reminiscent of 1983 in terms of opportunities lost. In the end, no championships were won – but an impressive victory at Silverstone made up for it in part. Here the winning XJR-6 of Cheever and Warwick crosses the line at the end of 1000 very satisfying kilometres. The other car, driven by Brancatelli and Schlesser, was all set to come second until time was lost fixing a gear-linkage which had pulled out. Although it performed a formation finish, car No.52 was in fact placed seventh overall.

SILK CUT
JAGUAR
51 SILK CUT
JAGUAR
DUNLOP

Mobil
Lucas
GROUP LTD
KOUROS
Shell Oils
JAGUAR
51
52
Castrol

Tom Walkinshaw takes his medicine . . . and is 'comforted' by Eddie Cheever and Derek Warwick, Silverstone, May 1986. TWR's first Group C hurdle has been vaulted.

Today, Silverstone.
JAGUAR
Le Mans, France.
31st May — 1st June
Norisring, Germany.
29th June
Brands Hatch,
Great Britain.
20th July
Nürburgring, Germany.
24th August
Tomorrow, the World.
Spa Francorchamps,
Belgium.
14th September
Fuji, Japan.
5th October
Selangor, Malaysia.
30th November
Surfers Paradise,
Australia.
7th December
Calendar of races correct at time of going to press.
The Jaguar XJR-6 6.0 litre V12. Maximum speed, 230 mph. Driven by Derek Warwick, Eddie Cheever, Jean-Louis Schlesser, Gian-Franco Brancatelli, and 50 years of racing achievement.
Castrol
JAGUAR The legend grows

"Today Silverstone . . . tomorrow the World." Jaguar's post-race advertising could not be more prophetic. Shortly afterwards John Egan – head of a company now breaking all its previous business records – was knighted in the Queen's Birthday Honours List.

Thirty TWR Jaguar Victories, 1982-1987

GROUP A

1982
Zolder, Belgium*
Brno, Czechoslovakia
Nürburgring, W. Germany
Silverstone (T.T.) England
Zolder, Belgium

1983
Donington Park, England
Pergusa, Sicily
Brno, Czechoslovakia
Zeltweg, Austria
Salzburg, Austria
Hockenheim, W. Germany*

1984
Monza, Italy
Donington Park, England
Pergusa, Sicily
Brno, Czechoslovakia
Zeltweg, Austria
Salzburg, Austria
Francorchamps (24-hr), Belgium
Macau, China*

1985
Bathurst (1000 km), Australia*

GROUP C

1986
Silverstone, England
Nürburgring, W. Germany

1987
Jarama, Spain
Jerez, Spain
Monza Italy
Silverstone, England
Brands Hatch, England
Nürburgring, W. Germany
Francorchamps, Belgium
Fuji, Japan

*All group A races listed were won by Jaguar XJ-S V12-engined coupés. All were rounds of the European Touring Car Championship, except those marked thus:**

All Group C races listed were won by XJR-6 (1986) and XJR-8 (1987) V12-engined prototypes. All were rounds of the World Sports-Prototype Championship, except the 1986 German Supercup race at Nürburgring.

TWR's Jaguar Drivers

No fewer than twenty-six drivers, of twelve nationalities, raced TWR Jaguars during the team's first six seasons – 1982 to 1987. Others practised and/or tested cars, but only those actually taking part in a competition proper are listed here. Best TWR Jaguar placings (1st, 2nd, or 3rd) are included individually. I have listed the drivers alphabetically, for reference rather than preference:

JEFF ALLAM (born Surrey, UK, 1954) is best known for his tenacious Rover Vitesse driving in Group A, culminating in a great 1986 Silverstone Tourist Trophy victory with Dennis Hulme. When a second XJ-S was added to the TWR-Motul-Akai team for the last three races of 1982, Allam drove on each occasion, retiring at Spa (with Dieudonné and Lovett) but finishing second to his team leader in last two rounds. His only other Jaguar drive came three years later at Bathurst, where his TWR-JRA XJ-S was squeezed by Allan Grice's Holden Commodore at the first corner. The car was withdrawn (from second place) immediately – almost certainly due to headlamp glass ingestion – thus depriving Australian Ron Dickson of a place in this listing. Allam's results for Jaguar were:

* *2nd in 1982 at Silverstone, with Lovett, (XJ-S)*
* *2nd in 1982 at Zolder, with Dieudonné (XJ-S)*

1987's World Sports-Prototype Champion driver, Raul Boesel.

RAUL BOESEL (born Brazil, 1957) had no ideas about driving for the Silk Cut Jaguar Team when he was resident in the USA in 1986, having put Formula One behind him for the moment; then Eddie Cheever chatted to him, and consequently he phoned Coventry and Kidlington at just the right time. A test drive led to his adoption as Derek Warwick's effective replacement alongside Cheever for 1987. In this, his first season, thanks to Cheever, Nielsen, Brundle, Dumfries and his own maturity and brilliance – sometimes barely contained, as when he spun at Monza and Brands Hatch – Boesel became the first Jaguar drive ever to win a World title, thus:

* *3rd in 1987 at Jarama, with Cheever (XJR-8)*
* *1st in 1987 at Jerez, with Cheever (XJR-8)*
* *1st in 1987 at Silverstone, with Cheever (XJR-8)*
* *3rd in 1987 at Hockenheim (Super Cup), solo (XJR-8)*
* *1st in 1987 at Brands Hatch, with Nielsen (XJR-8)*
* *1st in 1987 at Nürburgring, with Cheever (XJR-8)*
* *1st in 1987 at Spa-Francorchamps, with Brundle and Dumfries (XJR-8)*
* *2nd in 1987 at Fuji, with Dumfries (XJR-8)*

Gianfranco Brancatelli, a member of the 1986 Group C team.

GIANFRANCO BRANCATELLI (born Italy, 1950) won the 1985 European Touring Car Championship for Volvo assisted by Thomas Lindström. His first success was in 1974, when he was *Formula Italia* champion. This was followed by two successful seasons in Formula 3; then two unsuccessful ones, still with single-seaters (which happened to be unreliable *and* uncompetitive). After two years away from the sport, he returned in 1982 – the first Group 'A' year. In 1982 and 1983 his fiery driving gave Alfa Romeo many a class-victory and 1984 brought him two outstanding wins – Nürburgring and the Silverstone TT – sharing the work with Helmet Kelleners in the Eggenberger BMW-Italia 635CSi. 1985 confirmed his brilliance in the series, battling against Tom Walkinshaw, who chose him for his Group C team following some memorable encounters. In 1986, the wiry Italian contributed strongly to TWR's Group A (Rover) assault on the Touring Car Championship, as well as to the Group C (Jaguar) programme. His XJR-6 results 'on paper' – sixth at Brands Hatch and seventh at Silverstone – did him less than justice. In 1987, however, he was back in the area where he had proved himself – Group A – and was winning again for BMW.

MARTIN BRUNDLE (born Norfolk, UK, 1959) may have been the frustrated star of the Formula One firmament, first with Tyrrell – where it would have paid him to stay – and then with Zakspeed, who had seemed to be improving in 1986. In 1987, however, the small German team continued to be an 'also-ran', and the young Kings Lynn driver lost his lighthearted look. It did reappear at Spa-Francorchamps in September when he set up Raul Boesel's World title. Brundle had been a Walkinshaw protégé before his highly successful Formula Three period. He has a fine race record

Seen with Tom Walkinshaw at Monza in 1984 and with Roger Silman at Spa-Francorchamps in 1987, Martin Brundle is the only member of the TWR Jaguar team to have won with both the XJ-S and the Group C car.

under the TWR banner, despite being an irregular member of the Group A and Group C teams due to his Formula One commitments, and made history by putting the XJR-6 ahead of the field in its very first race. Soon afterwards, Ken Tyrrell banned him from Group C, following the death of his Formula One team-mate Stefan Bellof. He returned to TWR for three races in 1987.

* *1st in 1983 at Donington, with Calderari and Fitzpatrick (XJ-S)*
* *1st in 1983 at Zeltweg, with Walkinshaw (XJ-S)*
* *1st in 1984 at Pergusa, with Calderari (XJ-S)*
* *3rd in 1985 at Mosport, with Schlesser and Thackwell (XJR-6)*
* *1st in 1987 at Spa-Francorchamps, with Boesel and Dumfries (XJR-8)*

Enzo Calderari, swift Swiss from Biel, three times a winner with the XJ-S.

ENZO CALDERARI (born Switzerland, 1953) has established himself as a fast and reliable team man, especially in Group A touring cars. He was a regular member of the TWR-Motul Jaguar team in 1983 and 1984, and scored a number of useful results. He stayed with touring car racing after the Jaguars had departed, and (with Fabio Mancini and a BMW M3) scored a fine victory in the 1987 Silverstone TT, run in pouring rain. These were his main Jaguar achievements:

* *1st in 1983 at Donington, with Brundle and Fitzpatrick (XJ-S)*
* *2nd in 1983 at Zeltweg, with Dieudonné (XJ-S)*
* *1st in 1983 at Hockenheim (national), solo (XJ-S)*
* *1st in 1984 at Pergusa, with Brundle (XJ-S)*

* *3rd in 1984 at Brno, with Sears (XJ-S)*
* *2nd in 1984 at Salzburg, with Sears (XJ-S)*
* *2nd in 1984 at Silverstone, with Sears (XJ-S)*

EDDIE CHEEVER (born USA, 1958) has lived in Europe for most of his life. He was 14 when he began racing karts, and was winning in F3 and F2 while still a teenager. Throughout the eighties he has become a star of prototype racing with Lancia, and F1 with a variety of teams. His runner-up results at Detroit for Ligier in 1982 and at Montreal for Renault in 1983 put him clearly in the top rank. 1984 and 1985 did not bring such success, however, but an impressive one-off Lola drive in 1986 led to a regular position with Arrows, and 1987 restored him to a position in the top twelve Grand Prix points-scorers. Meantime, Tom Walkinshaw had made a good move, signing Cheever for the 1986 Silk Cut Jaguar Team and being rewarded with the XJR-6's only two victories. But for the priority of Grand Prix racing when dates clashed, Eddie Cheever could have shared the World Group C title with Raul Boesel. Consistently quick, Cheever scored five outright victories in two seasons of Group C:
* *1st in 1986 at Silverstone, with Warwick (XJR-6)*
* *1st in 1986 at Nürburgring (Super Cup), solo (XJR-6)*
* *3rd in 1987 at Jarama, with Boesel (XJR-8)*
* *1st in 1987 at Jerez, with Boesel (XJR-8)*
* *1st in 1987 at Silverstone, with Boesel (XJR-8)*
* *1st in 1987 at Nürburgring, with Boesel (XJR-8)*

Solo victory for Eddie Cheever with the XJR-6 at the Nürburgring, in the final of the 1986 German Supercup series . . .

. . . and afterwards with two of the fastest Group C Porsche drivers, Klaus Ludwig and (left) Hans-Joachim Stuck – second in this event, but Supercup series winner in 1986 and 1987.

PIERRE DIEUDONNÉ (born Belgium, 1947), in the tradition of his compatriot Paul Frére, is a writer as well as a race-driver. He has track-tested some great cars, including the XJR-6, and has taken part in many forms of racing; but touring car events are his speciality, and he has been with top teams regularly since becoming co-winner of the European Touring Championship for BMW in 1976. In 1987 he and Steve Soper won at Bathurst and Calder for Ford. Back in 1981, he won the Belgian 24-hour race with Tom Walkinshaw in a Mazda RX7; he joined the TWR-Motul Jaguar Group A team when it got its second car a year later, and stayed on in 1983. These were his best Jaguar placings:
* *2nd in 1982 at Zolder, with Allam (XJ-S)*
* *3rd in 1983 at Vallelunga, with Walkinshaw and 'Nicholson' (XJ-S)*
* *2nd in 1983 at Zeltweg, with Calderari (XJ-S)*

Pierre Dieudonné, Jaguar Group A team member, 1982-83.

'JOHNNY DUMFRIES' (born Scotland, 1958) leapt to fame by winning the 1984 British Formula Three championship in a Dave Price Ralt-VW. In 1986 he found himself elevated to Formula One with Lotus, but playing second fiddle to Ayrton Senna. When politics took over and the engine supplier (Honda) demanded that a Japanese (Nakajima) should replace him, Dumfries could have been out in the cold. On the contrary, the man who prefers not to use his title (he is in fact the Earl of Dumfries) kept his own cool, and 1987 turned into a great year for him with victories in IMSA and

New boy at Spa-Francorchamps, Johnny Dumfries, made good after a practice crash. Roger Silman, Silk Cut Jaguar Team director, does not look quite as pleased with him as does Ron Elkins or Sir John Egan.

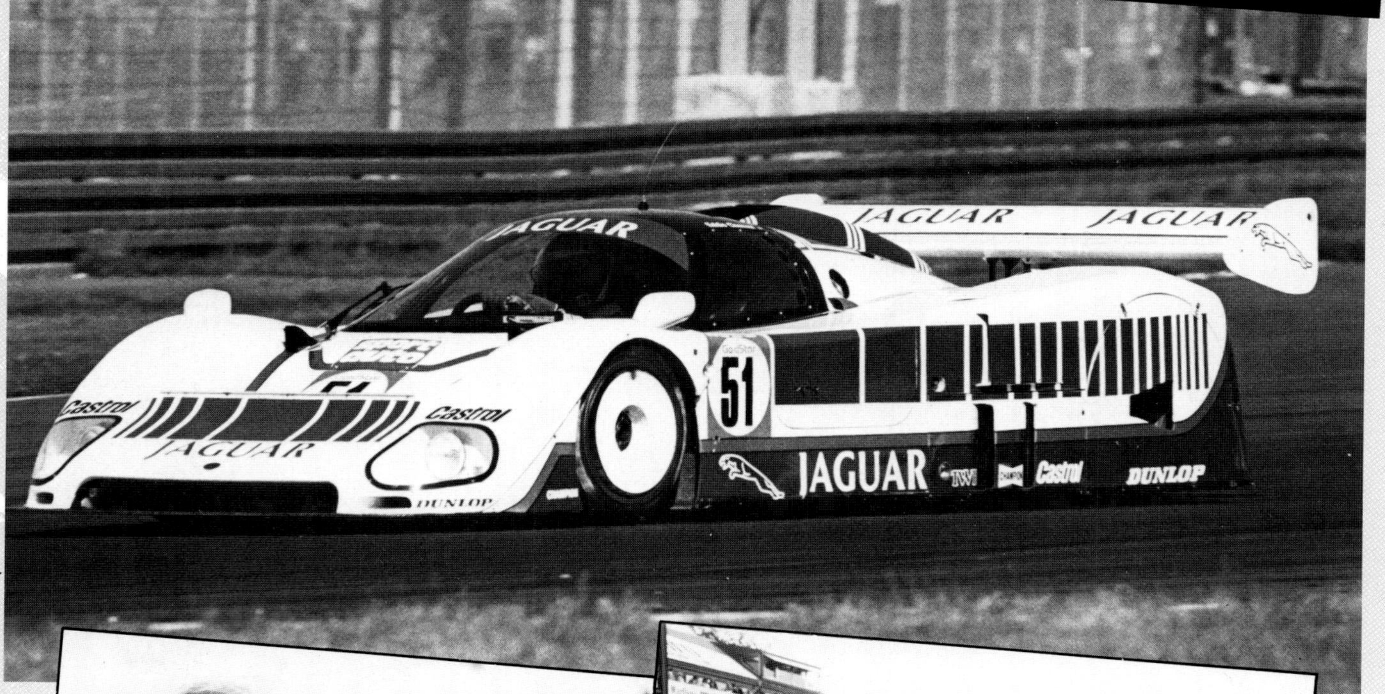

JAGUAR
Castrol
51
DUNLOP

sport auto
Das Magazin für Autofans
GoldStar
JAGUAR
Castrol
BLAUPUNKT
swatch

Castrol
TOWNSEND THORESEN

Group C, plus the chance to show his ability in the Sauber-Mercedes, the Porsche 962, and the Jaguar XJR-8 with which he won, first time out (to make up for an 'off' in practice):

* *1st in 1987 at Spa-Francorchamps, with Boesel and Brundle (XJR-8)*
* *2nd in 1987 at Fuji, with Boesel (XJR-8)*

John Fitzpatrick, briefly a TWR team member in 1983.

JOHN FITZPATRICK (born UK, 1944) – a 'founder-member' of the Broadspeed team – was a British saloon car champion in the 1960s, and went on to greater things. In 1976, when he won a thrilling World Championship six-hour race at Silverstone with the Group 5 BMW CSL, his co-driver was Tom Walkinshaw. Fitzpatrick drove with verve for the unsuccessful British Leyland Broadspeed XJ12 team in 1977. He won the IMSA Camel series in 1980 and, although involved in running his own team in Group C, joined the TWR Jaguar Group A team for 1983; but he fell out with Walkinshaw that summer and left. Before giving up racing, Fitzpatrick scored one last big win, in the 1983 Brands Hatch 1000 km race co-driving a Group C Porsche 956 with Derek Warwick. His brief Group A Jaguar stint brought him the following:

* *1st in 1983 at Donington, with Brundle and Calderari (XJ-S)*
* *3rd in 1983 at Mugello, with Walkinshaw (XJ-S)*

John Goss, whose career began with a Holden in Tasmania in the early sixties.

JOHN GOSS (born Australia, 1943) had raced Ford Falcons throughout the 1970s, the highlight being his victory in the 1974 Bathurst classic, achieved with assistance from Kevin Bartlett. (Goss made it a remarkable double that year, also winning the Australian GP for single-seaters.) The early 1980s saw Goss make several unsuccessful attempts to develop his own Jaguar XJ-S into a winner Down Under, and in 1984 – after breaking the clutch of Goss's car and being rammed from behind on the starting line – Tom Walkinshaw promised the Australian a drive in a TWR car at Bathurst the following year. The result was historic:

* *1st in 1985 at Bathurst, with Hahne (XJ-S)*

ARMIN HAHNE (born Germany, 1955) has a fine record in long-distance touring car racing with Ford, BMW, Jaguar and Rover. He has won the two most important events in this category – the 24 Hours of Francorchamps and the James Hardie 1000, the latter success being achieved in 1985 in a TWR Jaguar XJ-S with John Goss co-driving. Despite being brought in at the last minute (when Ivan Capelli ran into team-contract trouble) the popular German proved himself well able to cope with the change of environment at Le Mans where he co-drove with Brancatelli and Percy in 1986, in one of three XJR-6s. He returned to the TWR-Jaguar team for its last three appearances in Group A, giving the five-year old XJ-S a resounding second place in its final event. Hahne's Jaguar achievements, in a nutshell, are:

* *1st in 1985 at Bathurst, with Goss (XJ-S)*
* *2nd in 1987 at Pukekohe, with Percy (XJ-S)*

On stage: Armin Hahne sharing the 1985 Bathurst podium with John Goss and (extreme left) the Hon. Gerald Lascelles, Grand Master of this great event.

Backstage: Armin Hahne drove in practice, but didn't get to race at Le Mans in 1987. He chats to journo Graham Smith philisophically, while Chris Tuckey of TWR gets rid of excess rainwater from the lean-to roof.

HURLEY HAYWOOD (born USA, 1948) lives in Ponte Vedra, Florida, and has been a consistent winner in IMSA GT racing since it began in 1971. He won Le Mans driving Porsches in 1977 and 1983. Soon after the latter event he was injured in an accident. Despite a foot which took a long time to heal, he joined Bob Tullius's Group 44 Jaguar IMSA team in 1984, and won at Road Atlanta in 1985 with Brian Redman, in the Dykstra-designed V12-engined XJR-5. He finished third in that year's IMSA GTP points standings, beaten only by Porsche drivers Al Holbert and Derek Bell. 1986 was a leaner year for Group 44; but, in the team's winding-down season (1987), Hurley Haywood and John Morton took the updated car (the XJR-7) to stirring victories in the Riverside and Palm Beach IMSA rounds. Having won twice at Le Mans, and competed there in 1985 for Group 44, Haywood was a natural selection for the nine-driver squad when TWR made its first, unsuccessful, bid in the French marathon in 1986.

Hurley Haywood, a leading IMSA driver since the association was formed, and a TWR Le Mans driver in 1986.

HANS HEYER (born Germany, 1943) has an excellent record in touring car racing. He was European Champion for Ford in 1974 and, but for a quirk of the regulations, he would have shared the championship again in 1984 – the year in which he co-drove the TWR-XJ-S with Tom Walkinshaw. (As things turned out Tom was first and Hans was second). A regular winner of the Francorchamps 24-hour race, Hans Heyer has also scored some fine sports-prototype victories, including Imola (Lancia) in 1983 and Sebring (Porsche) in 1984. He was selected by Tom Walkinshaw for the original (1985) XJR-6 team and has been an occasional member of the squad subsequently. He shared the Haywood/Redman Silk Cut Jaguar Team car No. 52 at Le Mans in 1986. His greatest Jaguar successes were:

* *1st in 1984 at Monza, with Walkinshaw (XJ-S)*
* *3rd in 1984 at Vallelunga, with Walkinshaw (XJ-S)*
* *2nd in 1984 at Pergusa, with Walkinshaw (XJ-S)*
* *1st in 1984 at Brno, with Walkinshaw (XJ-S)*
* *1st in 1984 at Zeltweg, with Walkinshaw (XJ-S)*

Hans Heyer, his famous hat, and the XJ-S which he drove to four victories in 1984.

* *1st in 1984 at Spa-Francorchamps, with Percy and Walkinshaw (XJ-S)*
* *2nd in 1984 at Macau (non-chsp), solo (XJ-S)*

DENNIS HULME (born New Zealand, 1936) is, truly, a legend in his own lifetime. He has starred in single-seaters, sports cars and saloons and was Formula One World Champion for Brabham in 1967. He won his first Tourist Trophy in 1965 in a Brabham-Climax and (with Jeff Allam to help him) did it again in a Rover Vitesse twenty-one years later. In his early days, Denny Hulme usually drove Coopers, but among his victories was the 1963 Brands Hatch six-hour race with Roy Salvadori in a 3.8-litre Jaguar Mark 2. When Tom Walkinshaw extended the life of his Group A Jaguars to run at Fuji in 1986 and Wellington in 1987, Hulme was invited to co-drive with Armin Hahne. It was not the fault of either of them that they did not finish either race. Hulme made up for this by joining Larry Perkins (Holden Commodore) to win at Pukekohe in February 1987. A remarkable man.

Denny Hulme after his great Rover Vitesse win in the 1986 TT. He raced Jaguars in 1963 and in 1986/7.

ALAN JONES (born Australia, 1946) is the other former GP World Champion (1980) who has piloted a Jaguar for TWR. He drove an XJR-6 once – at Brands Hatch in 1985, before the new Group C team had established a regular squad – but did not finish. (Alan Jones's father, Stan, was a fine driver, too, and at one time raced a Cooper-Jaguar.)

JAN LAMMERS (born Holland, 1956) has proved his pace on many occasions. He and Jonathan Palmer won the 1984 Brands Hatch Group C race in the Lloyd Porsche 956, and shared sixth place in that year's World Endurance Championship. He raced with the TWR Jaguar Group C team in 1985 at Brands Hatch and Selangor, contributing greatly to the newcomer's best result of the year at the latter event. However, he did not become a regular Silk Cut Jaguar driver until 1987 when, with John Watson as his regular co-driver, he put in some wonderful performances for the team:
* *2nd in 1985 at Selangor, with Nielsen and Thackwell (XJR-6)*
* *Equal 2nd with John Watson in the 1987 WSC Championship*

Jan Lammers, a great team driver: mature, reliable and very fast.

* *1st in 1987 at Jarama, with Watson (XJR-8)*
* *1st in 1987 at Monza, with Watson, with Watson (XJR-8)*
* *3rd in 1987 at Brands Hatch, with Watson (XJR-8)*
* *2nd in 1987 at Spa-Francorchamps, with Watson (XJR-8)*
* *1st in 1987 at Fuji, with Watson (XJR-8)*

PETER LOVETT is best-known as a Rover man, but in 1982 he drove the new No. 2 TWR-Motul-Akai Jaguar XJ-S at Spa-Francorchamps and in the TT at Silverstone:

* *2nd in 1982 with Allam at Silverstone (XJ-S)*

'CHUCK NICHOLSON' was the *nom de course* of Lincolnshire businessman Charles Nickerson, whose rotary-engined Mazda RX7 was one of his links with Tom Walkinshaw. He had owned a rare Cunningham, and he had raced a Jaguar Mark VIII for fun – likewise he enjoyed a bit of rallying, usually in a Ford. At Spa-Francorchamps in 1981 Mazdas came first and fifth in the 24-hour race driven by Walkinshaw/Dieudonné and 'Nicholson'/Allam/Percy/Duez respectively, and things became more serious. When he and Walkinshaw won the TT in his Mazda that autumn, 'Nicholson' was looking ahead to Group A – the new touring car formula for 1982. He mentioned it to Walkinshaw, and found that he had thought of the same thing. Rather than have his own car prepared, 'Nicholson' joined the TWR/Jaguar Group A team. While he usually drove a single stint (of three) in these c.500 km races 'Chuck Nicholson' did play a very important role – although he tended to play it down.

'Chuck Nicholson' contributed no fewer than nine ETC victories for Jaguar.

* *3rd in 1982 at Vallelunga with Walkinshaw (XJ-S)*
* *1st in 1982 at Brno, with Walkinshaw (XJ-S)*
* *1st in 1982 at Nürburgring, with Walkinshaw (XJ-S)*
* *1st in 1982 at Silverstone, with Walkinshaw (XJ-S)*
* *1st in 1982 at Zolder, with Walkinshaw (XJ-S)*
* *2nd in 1983 at Monza, with Walkinshaw (XJ-S)*
* *3rd in 1983 at Vallelunga with Walkinshaw and Dieudonné (XJ-S)*
* *1st in 1983 at Pergusa with Walkinshaw (XJ-S)*
* *1st in 1983 at Brno with Walkinshaw (XJ-S)*
* *1st in 1983 at Salzburg with Walkinshaw (XJ-S)*
* *1st in 1984 at Donington with Percy (XJ-S)*
* *3rd in 1984 at Pergusa with Percy (XJ-S)*
* *2nd in 1984 with Brno with Percy (XJ-S)*
* *2nd in 1984 at Zeltweg with Percy (XJ-S)*
* *1st in 1984 at Salzburg with Percy (XJ-S)*

JOHN NIELSEN (born Denmark, 1956) was a contemporary of Martin Brundle and Johnny Dumfries in Formula Three and was victorious several times in 1983 and 1984. He won two Formula 3000 rounds in 1985, and finished fourth in the new championship for single-seaters. In 1985, too, he joined TWR for the last two Group C events of the year, and in the final he drove the runner-up XJR-6. In 1987 he proved himself much more than just the stand-in he appeared to be at first, and his businesslike performance at

John Nielsen, interviewed for LBC by Greg Strange after his 1987 Brands Hatch win.

Brands Hatch helped set Raul Boesel on course for the World Group C title. The personable Dane also shared fourth place with Cheever at Spa-Francorchamps.

* *2nd in 1985 at Selangor, with Lammers and Thackwell (XJR-6)*
* *1st in 1987 at Brands Hatch, with Boesel (XJR-8)*

WINSTON PERCY (born Dorset, UK, 1943) is one of the world's best and most adaptable long-distance race-drivers, well-known for his *espirit de corps*. He has won many UK championships, and scored the highest number of marks (driving TWR Rovers) in the 1986 European Touring Car Championship – which he was generally thought to have won until an anomoly in the 'discarded scores' system put him behind BMW's Roberto Ravaglia. He backed Tom Walkinshaw strongly in his Jaguar Group A days, too. He drove a TWR XJ-S in the Belgian 24-hour race three times, finally winning in 1984. He and Walkinshaw *should* have won at Bathurst in 1985. He drove the Group A Jaguar in its last two events in early 1987, and for the Silk Cut Jaguar Team at Le Mans in 1986 and 1987. On the latter occasion he was lucky to escape from a high-speed accident due to tyre deflation. He continues to enjoy racing in a variety of makes, and is much in demand by touring car teams.

* *1st in 1984 at Donington, with 'Nicholson' (XJ-S)*
* *3rd in 1984 at Pergusa, with 'Nicholson' (XJ-S)*
* *2nd in 1984 at Brno, with 'Nicholson' (XJ-S)*
* *2nd in 1984 at Zeltweg, with 'Nicholson' (XJ-S)*
* *1st in 1984 at Salzburg with 'Nicholson' (XJ-S)*
* *1st in 1984 at Spa-Francorchamps, with Walkinshaw and Heyer (XJ-S)*
* *3rd in 1985 at Bathurst, with Walkinshaw (XJ-S)*
* *2nd in 1987 at Pukekohe, with Hahne (XJ-S)*

Win Percy (with Dunlop's Bill Mack) at the launch of the author's book on Jaguar racing history, just ten days after his great escape at Le Mans in 1987.

BRIAN REDMAN (born Lancashire, UK, 1937) now lives in Florida. His first race was at Rufforth in 1959, when he drove a Morris Minor Traveller, but it was not until 1965 that he began to show his exceptional skill, when he drove the ex-Coombs lightweight E-type Jaguar to over a dozen victories. His sponsor, Charles Bridges, then acquired a Lola T70 which put Redman on the ladder of success. Although he tried his hand at F2 and F1 (he was third in the 1968 Spanish GP for Cooper), his real forte has been

Brian Redman: two generations of Jaguar racing, including Group 44 and TWR at Le Mans.

endurance racing in sports-prototypes and he has won many of the classic events held on both sides of the Atlantic. He was a star driver for JW/Gulf, and noted for his handling of the awesome Porsche 917. He was US Formula 5000 champion three times in the 1970s, and IMSA Camel GT champion in 1981, driving Porsches and Lola-Chevrolet. He drove Group 44's V12 Jaguar-powered IMSA GT prototype for three seasons, ending in 1986; his biggest XJR-5 successes were victories at Miami in 1984 (with Harry 'Doc' Bundy) and Road Atlanta in 1985 with Hurley Haywood. Like Haywood, he was drafted into the TWR team for its unsuccessful first assault on Le Mans with the XJR-6 in 1986.

JEAN-LOUIS SCHLESSER (born France, 1952) has a background of F3, F2 and saloons. He was 1978 French F3 champion, and had an impressive one-off F1 drive to sixth place in the 1983 Race of Champions at Brands Hatch. In 1984 he drove Rovers for TWR who seconded him into the Jaguar XJ-S team for Vallelunga and Donington. He shared in the XJR-6's successful début at Mosport in 1985, and appeared regularly with the Silk Cut Jaguar Team throughout 1986 when his failure to produce good results – as with Brancatelli – could not be attributed to him entirely. In a troubled season, he scored a fifth at Spa, a sixth at Brands Hatch, and a seventh at Silverstone (with Cheever, Warwick, and Brancatelli respectively) – not enough, apparently, to earn him a place with the team in 1987. He continued to drive with spasmodic brilliance: Alfa Romeo in Group A and Sauber-Mercedes V8 in Group C. His highpoint was a Supercup victory at the Nürburgring, to give the small Swiss Sauber team its one victory of the year.

* *3rd in 1985 at Mosport, with Brundle and Thackwell (XJR-6)*

Jean-Louis Schlesser with XJ-S at Vallelunga, 1984 . . .
. . . and (now a member of the rival Sauber-Mercedes team) with Tom Walkinshaw at Francorchamps in 1987.

DAVID SEARS (born Norfolk, UK, 1955), son of the former Jaguar driver Jack Sears, joined TWR for the latter part of 1984 and proved a mature and worthy team member. His best results were

* *3rd in 1984 at Brno, with Calderari (XJ-S)*
* *2nd in 1984 at Salzburg, with Calderari (XJ-S)*
* *2nd in 1984 at Silverstone, with Calderari (XJ-S)*

A 1984 TWR team driver, David Sears, meets former Jaguar racing chief 'Lofty' England at the Salzburgring.

MIKE THACKWELL (born New Zealand, 1961) shared the XJR-6 with Brundle and Schlesser on its début in August 1985. He had scored Formula 3000 victories already that year, and he went on to share in TWR's excellent end-of-season showing in Malaysia. However, he moved to the Kouros Sauber-Mercedes team for 1986, when he gave Group C a fillip and the Swiss marque its first outright Group C victory, at the Nürburging, with henri Pescarolo's help.
* *3rd in 1985 at Mosport, with Brundle and Schlesser (XJR-6)*
* *2nd in 1985 at Selangor, with Nielson and Lammers (XJR-6)*

TOM WALKINSHAW (born Scotland, 1946) still drives touring cars occasionally, but wisely resisted the temptation to go in for Group C racing when he set up his own sports-prototype team on Jaguar's behalf in 1985. After all, he had proved himself a driver of class many times before that – ever since his first race around Ingliston in an MG Midget at the age of nineteen. Ten years later he proved he had reached the top rank by winning the Group 5 six-hour race at Silverstone, with John Fitzpatrick in a BMW. Another year on (1977) saw him share victory in the Group 2 Tourist Trophy at the same venue with Dieter Quester, once again in a BMW CSL, defeating the BL-Broadspeed Jaguar Coupés. In due course Walkinshaw turned to the British marque himself, and set his sights on the European Touring Car Championship when it was given a new lease of life as 'Group A' from 1982. He was third to Helmut Kelleners and Umberto Grano that year and a close second to his former co-driver Dieter Quester in 1983. At last, in 1984, he beat all the BMW men and became the first Jaguar driver to win the European Touring Car Championship for twenty-one years. He continued to race the XJ-S once a year: in Australia (1985), Japan (1986), New Zealand (1987). Between 1985 and 1986, he and Win Percy scored eight ETC victories in the TWR Rover VItesse, but in 1987 Walkinshaw took more of a back seat – and sometimes he seemed itchy-footed about it. There was no questioning the fact that the chief was missing his motor racing. Even after six seasons of Group A, Walkinshaw was still the 'winningest' ETC driver and wanted to remain so.
* *3rd in 1982 at Vallelunga, with 'Nicholson' (XJ-S)*
* *1st in 1982 at Zolder (national), solo (XJ-S)*
* *1st in 1982 at Brno, with 'Nicholson' (XJ-S)*
* *2nd in 1982 at Zeltweg, solo (XJ-S)*

Mike Thackwell, who drove the XJR-6 regularly in 1985, seen at an early Donington test session.

Tom Walkinshaw with John Crawford (PR chief of Australian importers, JRA) at Bathurst 1985 and photographed by the author at Salzburg in 1984 – the year in which he became ETC champion

* *1st in 1982 at Nürburgring, with 'Nicholson' (XJ-S)*
* *1st in 1982 at Silverstone, with 'Nicholson' (XJ-S)*
* *1st in 1982 at Zolder, with 'Nicholson' (XJ-S)*
* *2nd in 1983 at Monza, with 'Nicholson' (XJ-S)*
* *3rd in 1983 at Vallelunga, with Dieudonné and 'Nicholson' (XJ-S)*
* *1st in 1983 at Pergusa, with 'Nicholson' (XJ-S)*
* *3rd in 1983 at Mugello, with Fitzpatrick (XJ-S)*
* *1st in 1983 at Brno, with 'Nicholson' (XJ-S)*
* *1st in 1983 at Zeltweg, with Brundle (XJ-S)*
* *1st in 1983 at Salzburg, with 'Nicholson' (XJ-S)*
* *1st in 1984 at Monza, with Heyer (XJ-S)*
* *3rd in 1984 at Vallelunga, with Heyer (XJ-S)*
* *2nd in 1984 at Pergusa, with Heyer (XJ-S)*
* *1st in 1984 at Brno, with Heyer (XJ-S)*
* *1st in 1984 at Zeltweg, with Heyer (XJ-S)*
* *1st in 1984 at Spa-Francorchamps, with Heyer and Percy (XJ-S)*
* *3rd in 1984 at Zolder, with Heyer (XJ-S)*
* *1st in 1984 at Macau (non-champ.), solo (XJ-S)*
* *3rd in 1985 at Bathurst, with Percy (XJ-S)*

DEREK WARWICK (born Hampshire, UK, 1954) was southern area karting champion at 12 before moving to stock-car racing. His exceptional talent made him British Champion in 1971 and World Champion in 1972. Later he worked his way through Formula Ford, F3 and F2 – winning at every stage. He was runner-up to team-mate Brian Henton for Toleman in the 1980 F2 European Championship: then he moved into F1 for three seasons with Toleman. Head-hunted for Renault at the peak of their achievement – for they had launched the 'turbo era' of Grand Prix racing – Warwick joined the French team as Cheever was leaving it. He came second in Belgium and Britain in 1984, but in 1985 the Renaults lost their 'edge' as other teams matched their technology and then surpassed it. Time moves quickly in F1, and Warwick was an unlucky victim. However,

Derek Warwick on the day he gave the Group C Jaguar its first victory, with Sales & Marketing Director Roger Putnam (Silverstone May 1986).

the popular Hampshire driver (who was to join the Brabham F1 team in mid-1986) had also proved himself to be a fine sports car driver, and he became a TWR man alongside Eddie Cheever, Jean-Louis Schlesser, and Gianfranco Brancatelli for 1986 – Jaguar's first 'Silk Cut' season. What a season it was! For Derek Warwick and the team it ended on a knife-edge. Was he the World's Sports Car Champion? Was Silk Cut-Jaguar the winning team? At first it looked like it. Then the organisers went and did their sums again. The answer: negative. Warwick had to settle for third place in the Drivers' Championship. He had always emphasised his personal ambitions: to succeed in Formula One. In 1987 – no longer contracted to TWR – he concentrated on those ambitions, driving the Arrows-Megatron alongside Eddie Cheever (who, being retained by TWR, had a busier and more fruitful year). The Cheever-Warwick victory with the XJR-6 will remain an important entry in the record of sports car racing. As well as the following top-three placings, Warwick was placed fourth at Brands Hatch with Jean-Louis Schlesser.

* *1st in 1986 at Silverstone, with Cheever (XJR-6)*
* *3rd in 1986 at Norisring, solo (XJR-6)*
* *3rd in 1986 at Jerez, with Lammers (XJR-6)*
* *2nd in 1986 at Spa-Francorchamps, with Lammers (XJR-6)*
* *3rd in 1986 at Fuji, with Cheever (XJR-6)*

JOHN WATSON (born Northern Ireland, 1946) has a worthy Formula One record with several GP wins to his credit. So, when he and the world's premier single-seaters gave each other up, he had the wisdom to be choosy about the rest of his racing career. In 1984 he drove for Group 44 at Le Mans, where neither XJR-5 finished. His best race of that season was a win with Stefan Bellof (Porsche 956) at Fuji. Promising IMSA drives with the March-BMW GTP car ended when the project was wrapped-up, unfulfilled, at the end of 1986. Thus the opportunity for Watson and Jaguar to get together for 1987 seemed tailor-made for success. Watson and his co-driver Jan Lammers were victorious right away, and led the

John Watson in discussion with Jaguar's Ron Elkins at a motor show . . .

. . . and with designer Tony Southgate and TWR's Gary Davies (left) at Jarama, 1987.

Championship after four rounds. They also won the final round and were runners-up to Boesel in the 1987 C1 championship. In November 1987 Watson received the BRDC's ERA Club Trophy. This is presented for the best performance by a Briton abroad, driving a British car.

* *1st in 1987 at Jarama, with Lammers (XJR-8)*
* *1st in 1987 at Monza, with Lammers (XJR-8)*
* *2nd in 1987 at Silverstone, with Lammers (XJR-8)*
* *3rd in 1987 at Brands Hatch, with Lammers (XJR-8)*
* *2nd in 1987 at Spa-Francorchamps, with Lammers (XJR-8)*
* *1st in 1987 at Fuji, with Lammers (XJR-8)*

TWR Jaguar drivers for 1988

With a schedule of some twenty-five races in IMSA and Group C including Le Mans, 1988 was expected to be a busy year for TWR and its drivers. The driver line-up for the year was announced on 14 January, just as this book went to press, but there remained some unsigned contracts for the IMSA series, due to the more complex contractural arrangements which exist in the USA.

Biggest news was that Martin Brundle had opted out of Formula One and would return to Jaguar for a full season in both series. Johnny Dumfries and John Nielsen would become regular drivers, and 1987 team members Raul Boesel, Eddie Cheever, Jan Lammers and John Watson would also be back for 1988. Boesel and Nielsen were scheduled to concentrate on IMSA racing, in which a definite new signing was that of Danny Sullivan – former winner of the Indianapolis 500-mile race. More drivers were due to be brought in for Le Mans.

Also in January 1988, TWR celebrated its first ten years of operations at Kidlington, Oxford, where the organisation by now occupied seven factory units – one of which witnessed a magnificent New Year party prior to being utilised for a new road-car project, managed by Paul Davis. (TWR by now employed well over 300 people.)

Castrol
JARAMA
JEREZ
MONZA
SILVERSTONE
LE MANS

4

THE 1987 WORLD SERIES

NORISRING

BRANDS HATCH

NURBURGRING

SPA-FRANCORCHAMPS

FUJI

ROUND 1

Jarama:
A Brilliant Start

Date: 22 March 1987
Venue: Jarama circuit, near Madrid, Spain
Approx. race distance: 360 km (1 lap = 3.31 km)
Weather: bright and dry

Result	Car	Main Sponsor	Team	Drivers	Laps
1st	6.9 Jaguar XJR-8	Silk Cut	TWR	Lammers/Watson	109
2nd	3.0 Porsche 962 turbo	Rothmans	Porsche	Stuck/Bell	109
3rd	6.9 Jaguar XJR-8	Silk Cut	TWR	Cheever/Boesel	109
4th	2.8 Porsche 962 turbo	Shell/Sachs	Kremer	Weidler/Nissen	106
5th	2.8 Porsche 962 turbo	Fortuna	Brun	Larrauri/Pareja	106
6th	2.8 Porsche 962 turbo	Torno	Brun	Brancatelli/Sigala	105

The 1986/7 winter modifications which had turned the Design Council Award Winning XJR-6 into the XJR-8 paid off handsomely, giving the Silk Cut Jaguar Team a psychological advantage at the start of the season. The two TWR cars occupied the front row, Eddie Cheever having lapped in 1m.14.54s. and Jan Lammers in 1m.14.69s. The Jaguars' great downforce on to the track – one of the most significant features of the Tony Southgate design – did much to offset the fact that, being naturally aspirated, they did not share their turbocharged rivals' ability to 'switch on' more power to achieve special lap times.

Unlike Formula One, in which there was a single tyre manufacturer (Goodyear), Group C featured several. Michelin had gained the upper hand in 1986, greatly helping Walter Brun's Porsches take the team title. It was clear that the title would be hard to defend because apart from other developments the works Porsche and Jaguar teams could now enjoy the benefit from the latest Dunlop tyre technology, incorporating that remarkable material-of-the-decade, Kevlar. Based on the cross-ply rather than the radial-ply principle, these tyres gave the Rothmans and Silk Cut teams a clear advantage at the outset. Hans Stuck was spectacular in

practice, but 1m.14.71s. left him on the second row, alongside Mauro Baldi (1m.16.37s.) in the newly-built 'British' Porsche 962 of Britten-Lloyd Racing, sponsored by Liqui Moly and shod by Goodyear.

Cheever led Lammers, in cars numbered 4 and 5 respectively in the early stages, while Stuck was charging through the field from a bad start – yet having to watch his fuel consumption read-out all the while, for current Group C racing is as much about completing the course on the fuel allowed as about sheer speed.

It was not long before Cheever began catching the non-works Porsches. The American was holding a comfortable lead when he was called in for an unscheduled stop to top up with oil. (There had been warning of a leak, which could have led to bearing starvation on the many tight bends.) Later in the race, Boesel and Bell had a long scrap which ended in the Porsche driver's favour; the Jaguar's nose touched the Porsche's tail in frustration several times, and then Boesel had to drop back with a fuelling problem, eventually to finish some ten seconds behind Bell. ***Here,*** the third-placed Jaguar comes up to lap the Brun Porsche of Massimo Sigala and former Silk Cut Jaguar team driver Gianfranco Brancatelli.

Jarama was a 'sprint race' – only 225 miles yet considerably longer than a modern Formula One Grand Prix – and cars running on schedule made only one pit stop, for fuel, new tyres and a driver change. The works Porsche completed these tasks quicker than the leading Jaguar, and John Watson found himself just behind Derek Bell as the race moved into its second half. The Porsche and the Jaguar ***(above right)*** seemed fairly evenly matched; but Watson dived ahead when Bell accidentally made space for him, and thereafter the Ulsterman was in command.

They don't
come much cooler than John
Watson who, having established a fifteen-second
advantage over Bell, decided to cruise for home despite an
adequate supply of fuel. With virtually no fuel to spare, Bell drove hard in
the final laps; but Watson was watching his mirror carefully and was still
1,64 seconds to the good as the chequered flag swept down.

Watson is seen crossing the line having just lapped the fourth-placed Porsche for the third time, with the flying factory Porsche trapped behind the Kremer car. Setting off to take the flag is Jonathan Palmer in the Liqui Moly Porsche which Mauro Baldi had kept in fourth place earlier on; Palmer had just suffered a puncture, and decided it would be best to make for the finish line rather than the pits. Baldi and Palmer were classified eighth, behind Brun and Jelinski in their Gaggia-sponsored Porsche.

Despite appearing, in turn, to tease the opposition, Jan Lammers and John Watson (seen happily brandishing the winners' trophy) scored a memorable first victory for the XJR-8 at Jarama.

Jaguar's first world title bid

Back in the 1950s, Jaguar's target was solely to win at Le Mans with a few other races included for practice or experience. The World Sports Car Championship was not introduced until 1953 and, when it was, Jaguar took little apparent notice of it – but it did win Le Mans five times.

Nowadays, championships mean more than individual races – except in the case of the twenty-four hours of Le Mans which, at the time of writing, has still to be won by a modern Jaguar race team. (There was determination in Kidlington and Coventry that this aim *would* be achieved, despite Porsche's apparent stranglehold.)

In the winter of 1986/87, the TWR team had tested exten-

sively on both sides of the Atlantic – mainly at Sebring in Florida (for the temperatures) and at Ricard near Marseilles. For 1987, there were two distinct models: the XJR-8 (which Tony Southgate whimsically dubbed the 'sprint' car although he had designed it for events of 1000 kilometres!) and the XJR-8LM which was created specifically for the long grind of Le Mans. There were many detail differences for the latter, including a tail and wing configuration designed with the notorious Mulsanne Straight in mind.

The rear wheels were unspatted largely to simplify pit-stop procedure. These pictures were taken at Ricard (which has a particularly long straight) during those murky pre-season simulation trials. Nothing – not even Ricard – can fully represent twenty-four hours of racing at Le Mans. Nevertheless, the improved performance achieved during the winter did justify the team's confidence for the 1987 season generally.

Above all the 'atmospheric' Jaguar V12 engine, as modified by Allan Scott of TWR, was proving capable of matching the turbocharged Porsche and Mercedes-Benz units for performance and beating them for economy under competitive conditions.

ROUND 2

Jerez: Survival of the Fittest

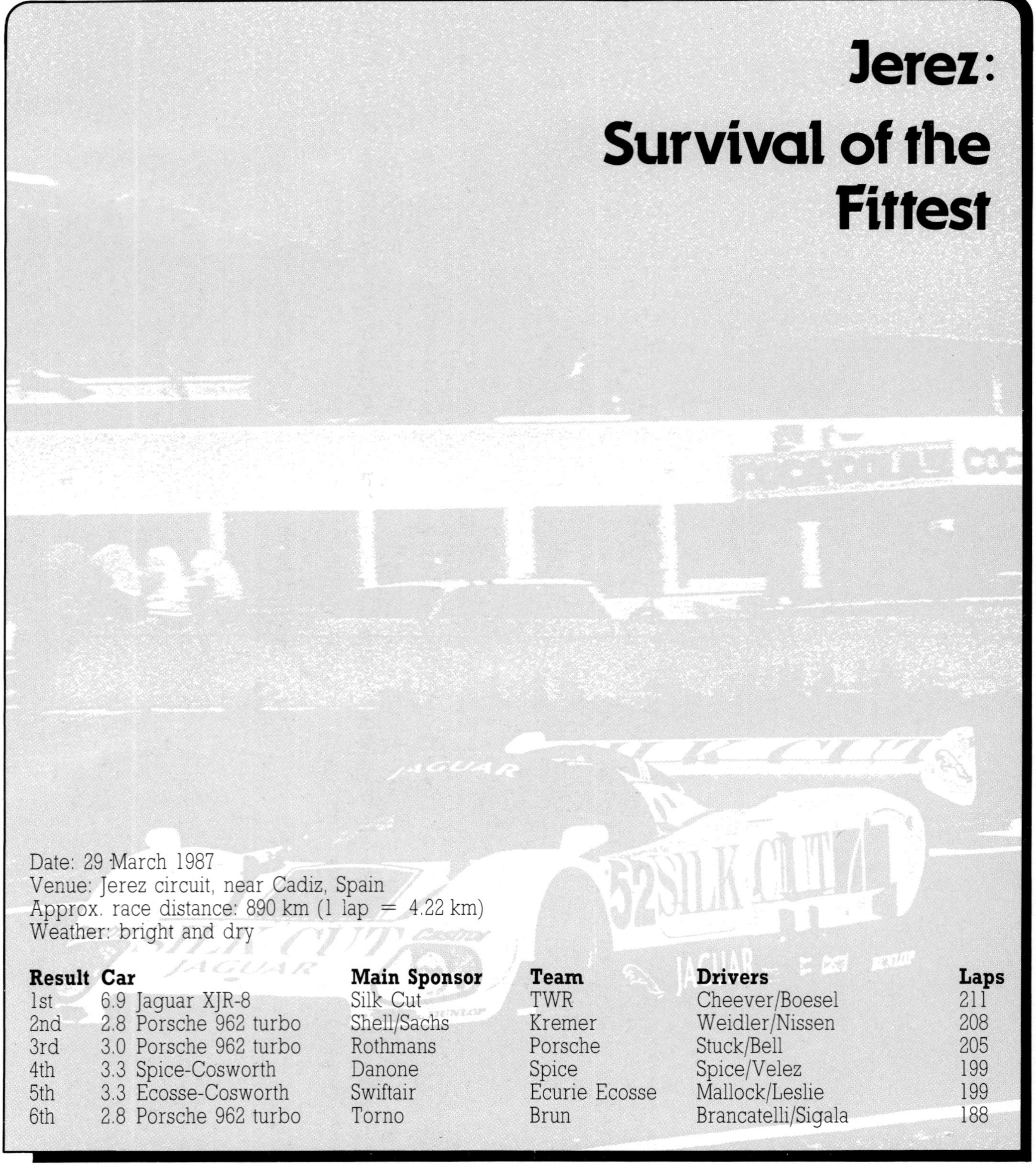

Date: 29 March 1987
Venue: Jerez circuit, near Cadiz, Spain
Approx. race distance: 890 km (1 lap = 4.22 km)
Weather: bright and dry

Result	Car	Main Sponsor	Team	Drivers	Laps
1st	6.9 Jaguar XJR-8	Silk Cut	TWR	Cheever/Boesel	211
2nd	2.8 Porsche 962 turbo	Shell/Sachs	Kremer	Weidler/Nissen	208
3rd	3.0 Porsche 962 turbo	Rothmans	Porsche	Stuck/Bell	205
4th	3.3 Spice-Cosworth	Danone	Spice	Spice/Velez	199
5th	3.3 Ecosse-Cosworth	Swiftair	Ecurie Ecosse	Mallock/Leslie	199
6th	2.8 Porsche 962 turbo	Torno	Brun	Brancatelli/Sigala	188

The Jerez circuit had witnessed a Group C race which spelled disaster for the Silk Cut Jaguar team's 1986 championship aspirations. In 1987 things did not begin too well either. For a start, it was clear to Tom Walkinshaw that the race would not run the full distance. (There is a rule which states that a '1000 km' race becomes an elapsed-time race at six hours – and Jerez is a 'slow' circuit.) However, his pending protest – that this situation would give the opposition a fuel consumption advantage – would not need airing afterwards, as things turned out. Another problem arose after Eddie Cheever failed to sign on, a technicality which saw him fined by the organisers. At any reasonable venue, someone would have made sure he did not practise until he *had* signed on, or at least have called him on the public address system. Cheever's front-row practice time of 1m.29.38s. was disallowed. Hans Stuck (1m.29.19s.) and Jan Lammers (1m.29.94s.) were the only other drivers to beat ninety seconds. The Rothmans v. Gallahers war was continued on the second row of the grid by Mass in a second works Porsche (1m.30.82s.) and Cheever who got there on the strength of 1m.32.93s. achieved by Boesel on race tyres rather than 'qualifiers'. Even earlier, Cheever had damaged the spare car against a wall. Maybe that is what he and his co-driver are looking so solemn about here.

Silk Cut
4
JAGUAR
DUNLOP
Castrol
TOWNSEND THORESEN

Silk Cut Silk Cut
TOWNSEND THORESEN
JAGUAR
Silk Cut
4
TOWNSEND THORESEN
Castrol
DUNLOP
JAGUAR
DUNLOP

Even on race day, the problems continued with the discovery of a gearbox breakage on car No. 5 with only just enough time to repair it before the start. Stuck, Lammers, Mass and Cheever ran nose-to-tail during the early laps, until Lammers suffered failure of a front stub axle; he came into the pits safely on three wheels, to spend close-on ten minutes immobile. After the first pitstops, the works Porsches now driven by Bob Wollek and Derek Bell led the XJR-8 of Raul Boesel, but not by much. John Watson was forced to abandon Jaguar No. 5 out on the circuit, however, with transmission failure – a fate which befell many cars including the Baldi/Palmer and Brun/Jelinski Porsches. Cheever had to go over a high kerb shortly before half-time, avoiding a back-marker who had not seen him coming, and the XJR-8 had to spend some time at rest while grass was removed and the bonnet-support brackets straightened up; in fact, another stop had to be made to strap No.4's bonnet on more securely *(see following photographs)*.

The Rothmans Porsches, however, (fitted with PDK double-clutch transmissions for this event) were in bigger trouble than the remaining Jaguar. The leading car of Mass and Wollek had transmission failure, while Stuck and Bell struggled on with both engine and gearbox in poor health – this tenacity rewarding them with third place. The only trouble-free Porsche was the Kremer car, and the leading C2 cars – the "Pontiac" of Gordon Spice and Fermin Velez and the Ecosse of Ray Mallock and David Leslie (both Cosworth DFL-powered) – were able to take high placings in the general order. But in the end, car No. 4 kept its strapped-up nose in place and had no difficulty in reeling off the final laps.

Shadows lengthen as No. 4 comes home a comfortable winner at Jerez. It was a great moment for Boesel who had not won anything lately, and (perhaps?) poetic justice for Cheever. They now led the drivers' championship with 32 points to the 27 of Bell and Stuck.

SILK CUT
DANONE
EXPO'92
52
JAGUAR
DUNLOP
N-17275
MICHELIN
SERVICE COMPETITION

Retrospective
In August 1986, the new Jerez circuit had hosted its first Group C race – a 360 km sprint which in the absence of the works Porsches, it seemed as though the Silk Cut Jaguar Team (with three cars) must be favourite to win. Unfortunately, Derek Warwick caused a first-corner accident involving himself and his team-mates Gianfranco Brancatelli and Eddie Cheever – *as illustrated in the first colour section of this book* – who had to make unscheduled pitstops while Warwick lost two laps digging himself out of a sandtrap. The other two XJR-6s eventually retired with drive-line failure – probably caused by series of bumps on the new course which had the cars jerking and jumping – while the Brun team laughed its way to a one-two finish. Lammers and a sheepish Warwick came third in car No. 52, seen here during practice, and *(inset)* while digging out.

There is not a very extensive history of sports-car racing in Spain, although Roy Salvadori and Ninian Sanderson *(Ecurie Ecosse* C-type Jaguars) did well to take second and third places to Picard's Ferrari in the 1954 Montjuich Cup race at Barcelona. Across the border in Portugal however, there were several historic moments for Jaguar drivers of the 1950s – notably Stirling Moss, Duncan Hamilton and Tommy Wisdom. Iberia's most important contribution to early Jaguar history took place more than half a century ago, though, when Casimiro de Oliveira won the international Vila Real road race for sports cars. This was the first international outright *race* victory for the marque anywhere. The winning 2.7-litre SS Jaguar 100 is seen during and after the event, in which the main opposition – as today – was German. An Adler was second and a BMW was third. In general, though, the SS Jaguar 100 was more suited to sprints and rallies, and William Lyons was known even to discourage private owners from racing their cars.

ROUND 3

Monza: Watson Wins—Boesel Blows It

Date: 12 April 1987
Venue: Monza circuit, near Milan, Italy
Approx. race distance: 1000 km (1 lap = 5.80 km)
Weather: sunshine, turning to cloud and rain

Result	Car	Main Sponsor	Team	Drivers	Laps
1st	6.9 Jaguar XJR-8	Silk Cut	TWR	Lammers/Watson	173
2nd	3.0 Porsche 962 turbo	Rothmans	Porsche	Stuck/Bell	171
3rd	2.8 Porsche 962 turbo	Fortuna	Brun	Larrauri/Jelinski/Pareja	168
4th	2.8 Porsche 962 turbo	Sachs	Joest	Ludwig/'Winter'/Dickens	167
5th	2.8 Porsche 962 turbo	Torno	Brun	Brancatelli/Sigala	165
6th	3.0 Porsche 962 turbo	Rothmans	Porsche	Mass/Wollek	159

Round Three was the first race of 1987 to clash with a Formula One Grand Prix, and this meant that Eddie Cheever's place in the Silk Cut Jaguar team would be taken by the personable Dane, John Nielsen, who had trained with the spare car at Jerez. (He had also driven the XJR-6 in 1985.) Not surprisingly, the turbocharged works Porsches out-qualified the two Jaguars at Monza, as did the Gaggia Porsche driven by Oscar Larrauri, whose scheduled co-driver was team chief Walter Brun. But ultra-fast laps are the prerogative of cars which can gain an instant power advantage through the application of turbo boost, and at no time did TWR risk race opportunities for the sake of a front row grid position. As it happened, no fewer than eight Porsche engines broke at Monza – *before* the race – a fact that led some team managers to blame the circuit's fuel supply. At the start, the Jaguars came forward from Rows 2 and 3 to do battle with the works Porsches. At first the order was: Stuck, Boesel, Wollek and Lammers, running in line astern. Having experienced XJR-8 performance twice already, the German team was all out to win this time (as it had done here in 1986, when the Silk Cut Jaguar Team made its début) to the extent that Porsche refitted its regular manual gearbox for the race. Stuck stayed

ahead until Lap 5, at which point Boesel overtook him to put Jaguar No. 4 ahead. Lammers attempted to do the same thing under braking for the Vialone chicane shortly afterwards, only to spin No. 5 to avoid the Porsche as Stuck stuck to his line. On Lap 10, Stuck suffered a puncture; Boesel and Wollek ***(seen here near the point where Lammers had spun)*** now occupied first and second places respectively.

Silk Cut Silk Cut
Silk Cut
JAGUAR
Silk Cut
5
JAGUAR
DUNLOP
SILK CUT
TOWNSEND THORESEN
Castrol
DUNLOP

Jan Lammers was quick to recover, bringing No. 5 up from sixth to third. On Lap 20 Bob Wollek went ahead. The scrap continued after the first pit-stops, with Mass leading Nielsen, and Watson. Nielsen led from Lap 36 to Lap 46. Then it was Mass from Watson (or Nielsen) until the next pit-stops.

Boesel's car ***(seen here)*** was the initial leader of this third session, but No. 5 went ahead on Lap 68. Wollek was there, still, taking second place from Boesel on Lap 80, but almost immediately the Alsace driver's Porsche suffered a turbocharger failure, losing many laps as the unit was replaced. Bell and Stuck remained competitive, but Bell lost time tangling with the Giacomelli/Baldi Liqui Moly Porsche, which had had to brake early (to miss Pareja's car) and which retired in due course when the rear wing fell off. Other Porsches were in trouble and Klaus Ludwig and Oscar Larrauri switched to other cars when their own failed.

The Jaguars were in charge for the second half of the race, with No. 5 (Watson/Lammers) controlling the pace as No. 4 (Boesel/Nielsen) began to lose its edge – though there seemed no danger of its losing a place. First and second for Jaguar was almost a racing certainty, as the wind got up and clouds scudded by. The first drops of rain fell with less than twenty minutes to go. Lammers did not hesitate, and came in at once for treaded Dunlops, shooting out into the spray without wasting time to have the wheelspats refitted. Boesel hesitated and was lost, deciding to do an extra lap treadless, and consequently leaving the course. Jaguar No. 4 had done 167 laps and, as Lammers took the chequered flag a few minutes later, it could still have been fourth – but it was stuck fast in the sand, an unhappy Boesel being awarded no marks by anyone that day. Thus the dogged Bell

and Stuck took second place, *and* the lead in the drivers' championship, much to Porsche's pleasure. Just afterwards, Porsche AG announced that it would be running its two-car team to challenge Jaguar for the rest of the season, except at the Norisring where Mass and Wollek were already committed to other cars. At Monza, Lammers recorded the fastest lap of the race.

Retrospective
Perhaps the most heroic Jaguar participation ever at Monza was in 1957 when *Ecurie Ecosse* founder David Murray entered three ex-works D-types for the 500-mile 'Race of Two Worlds'. The fully-banked circuit was used and the opposition was a specially-shipped group of Indianapolis-type single-seaters. Sticking to Dunlop's tyre-temperature limits (and running high on the banking to avoid scrub), the three cars ran steadily to 4th, 5th and 6th places as the American cars began to break up on the bumpy course. This picture shows Jack Fairman's Jaguar leading the whole field on the first lap. (The American cars had only two-speed gearboxes!) The eventual winner at about 160 mph was Jimmy Bryan in the Dean Van Lines Special (No.1). Fourth place went to Fairman at around 150 mph. His full, personal account of this remarkable event is included in *Jaguar Sport Racing and Works Competition Cars from 1954,* published in 1987 by G.T. Foulis & Co. Ltd.

ROUND 4

Silverstone: Jaguar 1 & 2; Mercedes Shows Its Hand

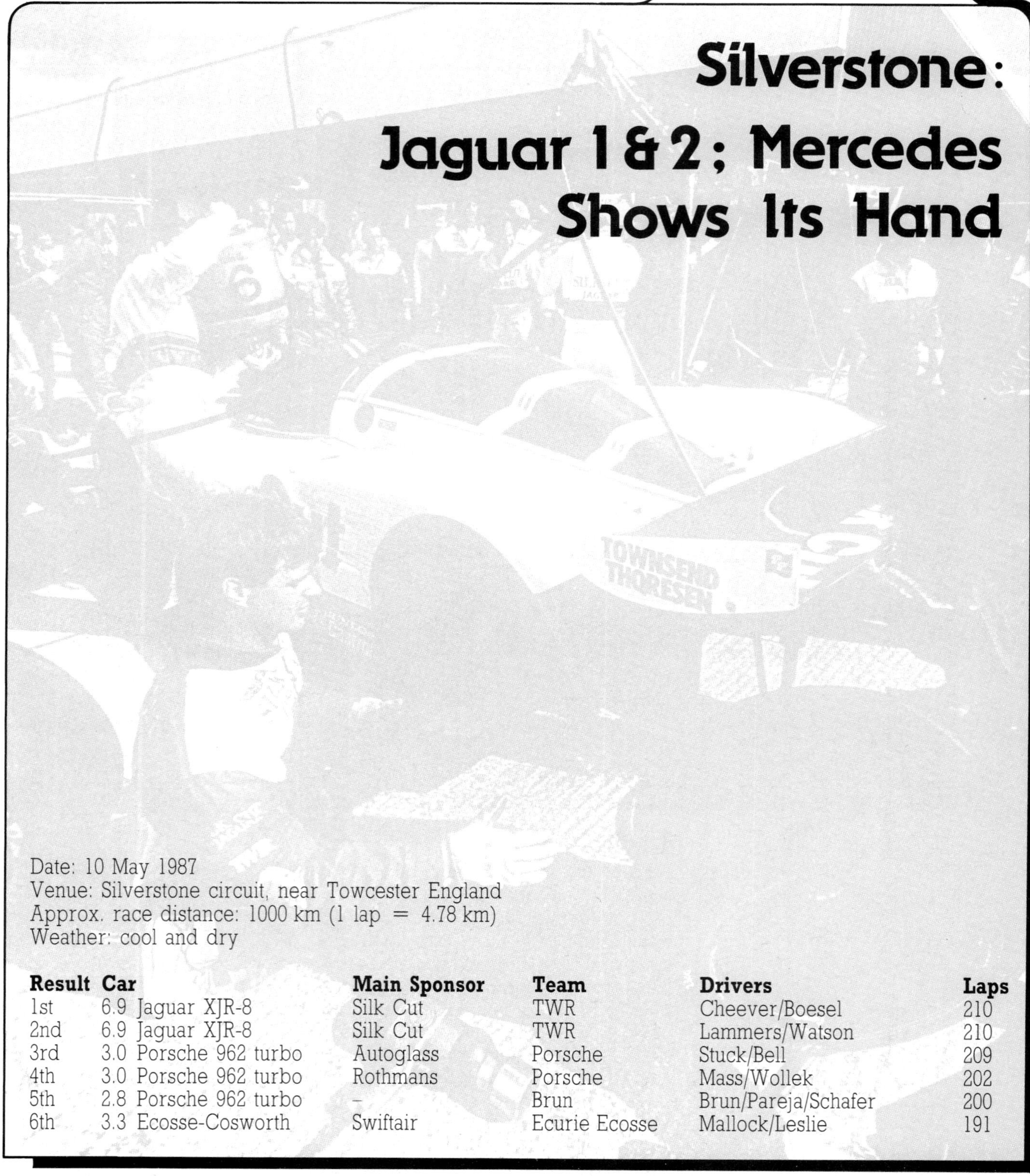

Date: 10 May 1987
Venue: Silverstone circuit, near Towcester England
Approx. race distance: 1000 km (1 lap = 4.78 km)
Weather: cool and dry

Result	Car	Main Sponsor	Team	Drivers	Laps
1st	6.9 Jaguar XJR-8	Silk Cut	TWR	Cheever/Boesel	210
2nd	6.9 Jaguar XJR-8	Silk Cut	TWR	Lammers/Watson	210
3rd	3.0 Porsche 962 turbo	Autoglass	Porsche	Stuck/Bell	209
4th	3.0 Porsche 962 turbo	Rothmans	Porsche	Mass/Wollek	202
5th	2.8 Porsche 962 turbo	–	Brun	Brun/Pareja/Schafer	200
6th	3.3 Ecosse-Cosworth	Swiftair	Ecurie Ecosse	Mallock/Leslie	191

Silverstone is Jaguar's home circuit, being within an hour's drive of the Coventry works. It was the venue for the original test of the Jaguar XK120 as a competition car, in early July 1949, after which William Lyons agreed to enter three works cars for the following month's production car race. It was to be the scene of many Jaguar triumphs, among them the first XJR-6 victory in 1986.

Before the 1987 Silverstone 1000 km, race, Duncan Hamilton and Tony Rolt demonstrated the actual (though rebodied) C-type Jaguar with which they had won Le Mans in 1953. In attendance were former Jaguar team chief 'Lofty' England and (wielding the chequered flag) race official Pierre Aumonier.

Sponsored by Autoglass, the 1987 event was the first long-distance event to be held on the newly-modified Silverstone circuit, with its sharp left-right bend designed to slow traffic before Woodcote Corner. This brought the number of laps down from 212 laps to 210 laps for 1000 km. It also meant that cars would now be passing along the pits straight at higher speeds than ever before, as Woodcote Corner no longer had a chicane.

With Le Mans in the offing, the Silk Cut Jaguar Team entered a third car (the new XJR-8LM) for Martin Brundle and John Nielsen, managed by Ken Page. It had less downforce and was trickier to handle than its team mates; tenth best with 1m.19.34s. seemed a fair début for a new car. *The* new car to watch at Silverstone was the C9 version of the Kouros Sauber-Mercedes with its 5-litre Mader-prepared turbocharged V8 engine, which sounded effortless once the car really got going towards the end of a troubled practice session. Although the windscreen made the car look familiar, its bonded aluminium construction had been modified considerably compared with the 1986 C8, and the small Swiss team had switched from Goodyear to Michelin tyres.

These helped the New Zealand-born Australian, Mike Thackwell, to startle the pit lane with a magnificent lap of 1m.15.17s. to put him alongside Hans Stuck who recorded 1m.15.11s. with the PDK-equipped works Porsche, carrying Autoglass and Shell sponsorship for this race. Mass took the other works car (with standard Rothmans insignia and 5-speed manual box) round in 1m.15.81s. compared with the best Jaguars' 1m.16.44s. for Cheever and 1m.16.62s. for Lammers.

Although the new corner was considered to put the Jaguars at a disadvantage, fourth and fifth on the grid seemed quite satisfactory. To the confidence of having won three races in a row was added the announcement that TWR would run Jaguar's IMSA programme in 1988 (with a different sponsor) while maintaining its commitment to a third year in the World Series with Gallaher International, proprietors of the 'Silk Cut' brand name which (unlike in 1986) *could* be displayed on the cars at Silverstone this time. The three Jaguars are seen lined up for the pits 'walkabout' which helps to bring the spectator closer to the action – an important factor, the car's and its cocooned driver's actions being so hard to see from beyond the barriers.

The Jaguar XJR-8LM with its flatter tail and open wheel arches was not part of the overall race plan. It was to be driven hard, this being its only race before Le Mans, to see if designer Tony Southgate could learn any last-minute lessons, and to familiarise Martin Brundle with it, of course. (The Norfolk driver had not raced a Jaguar for over twenty months.)

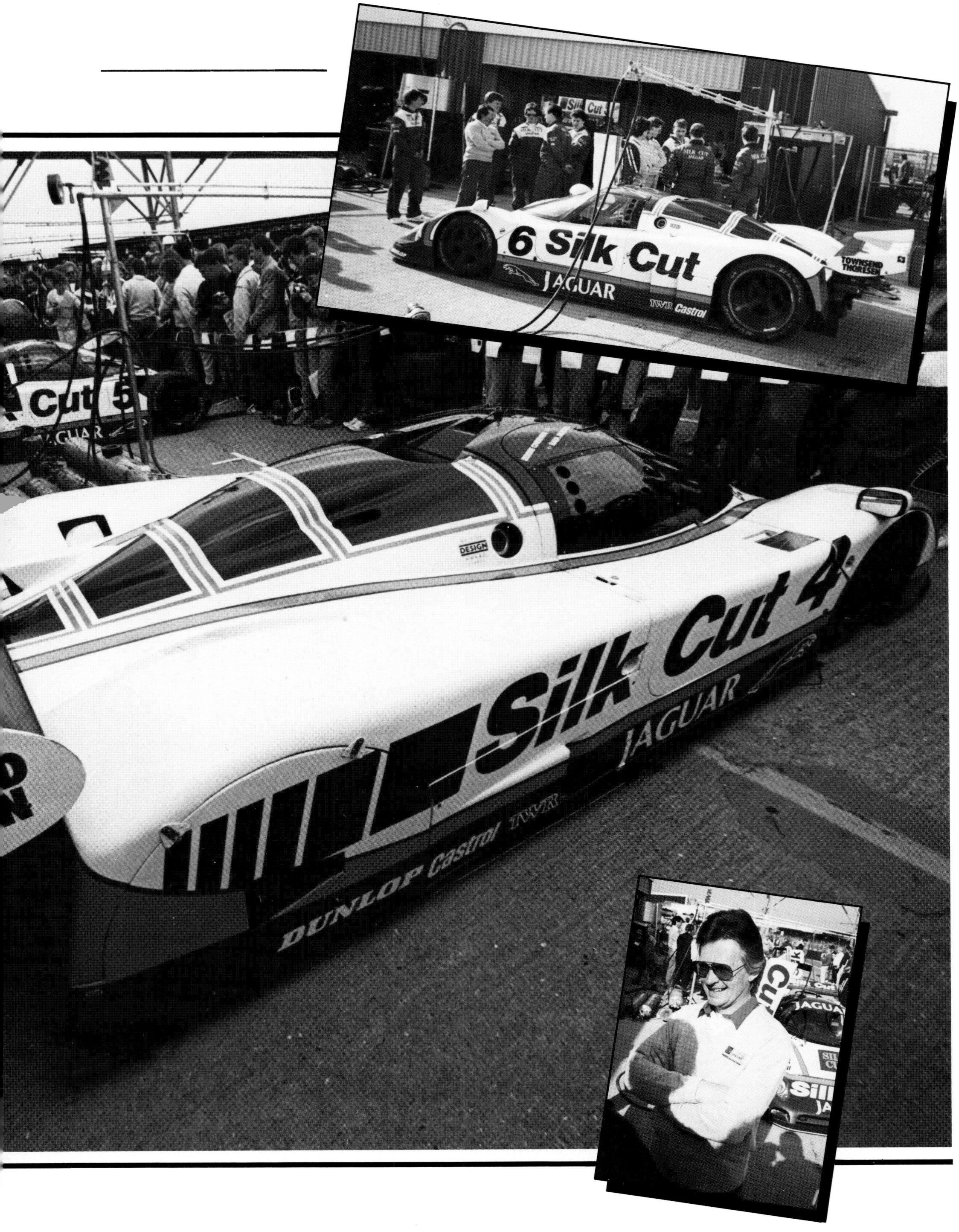
Silk Cut 4
JAGUAR
DUNLOP Castrol TWR
DUNLOP
Cut 5
JAGUAR
6 Silk Cut
JAGUAR
TWR Castrol
TOWNSEND THORESEN
JAGUAR

Former Jaguar driver Mike Thackwell jumped the gun at the rolling start, and who could blame him for his determination to put the new Sauber-Mercedes out in front at its first showing? The XJR-8s of Cheever and Lammers overwhelmed Stuck's PDK-Porsche almost at once, but it was not until Lap 17 that Cheever slipped into the lead in a braking manoeuvre. The American then drew away steadily, while Lammers made it a Jaguar one-two before the first scheduled pit-stops. This picture shows the XJR-8LM of Brundle and Nielsen, which was moving through the field well, too.

The Thackwell/Pescarolo Sauber-Mercedes began to misfire and, after sporadic reappearances, retired – but it made a great impression as a genuine rival to the Porsches and Jaguars. Jonathan Palmer's 'local' Liqui Moly car was one of several Porsches off-form at Silverstone, and after 50 laps the Jaguars were placed one, two, and three. Here, the Jaguar 'LM' accelerates out of the new S-bend before Woodcote Corner – not a universally-approved modification since it disturbs the flow of any high-speed lap of Silverstone.

6
TOWNSEND
THORESEN
TWR
121

The race settled down to being one of total Jaguar domination, although the LM car did have an altercation with a Porsche before retiring with low oil pressure and other problems. Had Nielsen over-revved? Generally, No. 4 led No. 5, but this changed when Boesel had a puncture and then stopped again to be on the safe side when the car felt peculiar. It was, simply, the effect of having hot and cold tyres on the same car – but, after blotting his copybook at Monza, the Brazilian was taking no unnecessary risks today. No. 4 got the upper hand again during the final pit-stops, when Lammers stalled No. 5's engine, and lost some time. The race was nearly over when the field was forced to line-up behind a pace car, while wreckage from an accident (no-one hurt) was cleared off the pit straight. This put the Jaguars close together for the last few minutes, and Cheever set a lap record of 1m.18.12s (nearly 137 mph, or 220 km/h.) Lammers played the dutiful team man and eased back slightly to hold station. The Jaguars crossed the finishing line six seconds apart.

Cheever and Boesel took the laurels, and made it four races in a row for Jaguar while, by finishing second, Lammers and Watson regained their lead in the Drivers' Championship. This is how the scoring looked:

Teams		**Drivers**	
Silk Cut Jaguar	80 pts	Watson & Lammers	55 pts
Porsche AG	54 pts	Bell & Stuck	54 pts
Brun Porsche	34 pts	Boesel & Cheever	52 pts

SILK CUT JAGUAR
SILK CUT
SILK CUT
JAGUAR
SILK CUT JAGUAR
SILK CUT
LK CUT
JAGUAR
Silk Cu
TOWNSEND THORESEN
4 Silk Cut
JAGUAR
DUNLOP

The Changing Face of Silverstone

The 1940s: Silverstone was first used for racing in 1948 and the perimeter circuit – essentially the present one of the just under three miles to the lap – was established for the 1949 season. At that year's International Trophy meeting sponsored by the *Daily Express,* the Formula One event was supplemented by Britain's first post-war race for production cars. Under pressure from the newspaper moguls, William Lyons was persuaded to enter three of his brand-new Jaguar XK120 sports cars as a flag-waving exercise. They were painted red, white and blue for the occasion. The blue car, driven by 'B. Bira', led but went off course with a puncture; the other two came first and second, handled by Leslie Johnson and Peter Walker, covering 28 laps in the allotted hour. Here Johnson's winning car can be seen leaving Abbey Curve, with the pits beyond. It was this result that opened the floodgates and, more or less, forced Jaguar to go motor racing with its own professional team.

The 1950s: By the time touring car racing was added to the programme, the Silverstone pits had been moved to their present general location, between Woodcote and Copse Corners. In this Guy Griffiths picture *(top right),* winner Stirling Moss dashes for his works Jaguar Mark VII as the inaugural (1952) event gets under way.

The 1960s: Jaguars dominated touring car racing for over a decade, and at Silverstone they were 'celebrity' events with big names bringing in the crowds and adding to the spectacle. This is the May 1960 race, when the 3.8-litre Mark 2 was the latest thing. The winner this time was Roy Salvadori (No.46) from Stirling Moss and Graham Hill. The friendly rivalry continued into the new 'GT' era, and the Woodcote corner photograph *(overleaf top)* shows the E-type Jaguars of Hill and Salvadori sandwiching Mike Parkes' Ferrari GTO in 1963. Parkes crashed and Hill won from Salvadori who set a new lap record.

BP
4 WPD

JOHN PLAYER GRAND PRIX
Motor
Leyland
1
Leyland
2

The 1970s: In this decade Jaguar was in no position to go motor racing in Europe; but British Leyland, of which Jaguar was a part, made arrangements for Ralph Broad to modify the XJ12 and race it against the all-powerful BMW CSL coupés in ETC Group 2 events. Overweight and overstressed, the 'Big Cats' always led spectacularly – but they never won. At Silverstone's TT races of 1976 and 1977 they were cheered to the echo, and on the latter occasion *(illustrated here)* the Jaguar of Derek Bell and Andy Rouse was closing on the leading Alpina CSL of Dieter Quester and Tom Walkinshaw, towards the end, when Rouse crashed. Within five years, however, Walkinshaw was the one proving that the V12 Jaguar engine had a lot to offer.

The 1980s: Driving a Motul Jaguar XJ-S, Tom Walkinshaw did win the first 'Group A' Tourist Trophy race at Silverstone in 1982, assisted by 'Chuck Nicholson'; but it was his team's victory in the 1000 Km sports-car race of 1986 that confirmed TWR's complete mastery of motor racing management at the highest level. He is seen with a jubilant Derek Warwick; they are greeting Eddie Cheever on his slowing-down lap after giving the XJR-6 its first-ever victory.

ROUND 5

Le Mans: Motor Racing is Dangerous

Date: 13/14 June 1987
Venue: La Sarthe circuit, near Le Mans
Race time: 24 hours (1 lap = 13.65 km)
Weather: damp to dry to wet to dry

Result	Car	Main Sponsor	Team	Drivers	Laps
1st	3.0 Porsche 962 turbo	Rothmans	Porsche	Stuck/Bell/Holbert	354
2nd	2.8 Porsche 962 turbo	Primagaz	Obermaier	Lässig/Yver/de Dryver	334
3rd	2.8 Cougar-Porsche turbo	Primagaz	Courage	Raphanel/Regout/Courage	331
4th	2.8 Porsche 962 turbo	Leyton House	Kremer	Fouche/Konrad/Taylor	326
5th	6.9 Jaguar XJR-8LM	Silk Cut	TWR	Cheever/Boesel/Lammers	324
6th	3.3 Spice-Cosworth	Dianetique	Spice	Spice/Velez/de Henning	320

Le Mans is fickle in every way. Words cannot express the annual drama and its dangers; nor can they explain why people abhor it, yet keep returning.

Le Mans had a fascination which attracted Jaguar in the 1950s, and led enthusiasts to demand the marque's return throughout a twenty-year absence from the entry lists. The modern assault was begun by Group 44 with two American-built V12-engined XJR-5 IMSA cars, and repeated the following year when one car finished – a troubled thirteenth.

In 1986 it was TWR's turn to try, with a three-car Silk Cut Jaguar Team; and, as with Group 44, it had no finishers the first time. For 1987 there was a determination to finish and – *possibly* – to win. The possibility was underlined by the experience of Porsche and its strength of numbers.

As in 1986, the Silk Cut Jaguar Team attended the test day at Le Mans. It was held on Sunday 17 May, the day after Coventry City FC – the 'Sky Blues' – made history by winning the Football Association Cup. Fans of the Jaguar marque, also from Coventry, flock to Le Mans in droves each year; and perhaps Boesel's BTD of 3m.24.38s. was seen as an omen? But the works Porsche of Bob Wollek was only a fraction of a second behind (3m.25.04s) – and lap times are not everything, especially when planning a high-speed run that is to last 24 hours. The unofficial session at Le Mans was most useful to Tony Southgate in checking the multitude of improvements he had incorporated since 1986. Most obvious was the change to the tail design, as first seen at Silverstone a week earlier. The traditional 'long-tail' theory had been thrown out in favour of a sharp cut-off to minimise vulnerability to damage by other cars. This and the open-wheel effect made the XJR-8LM look stubbier than its 1986 counterpart ***(shown here),*** but in fact over a month of testing in the wind-tunnel of London's Imperial College had shown Southgate other ways of reducing drag *and* increasing downforce.

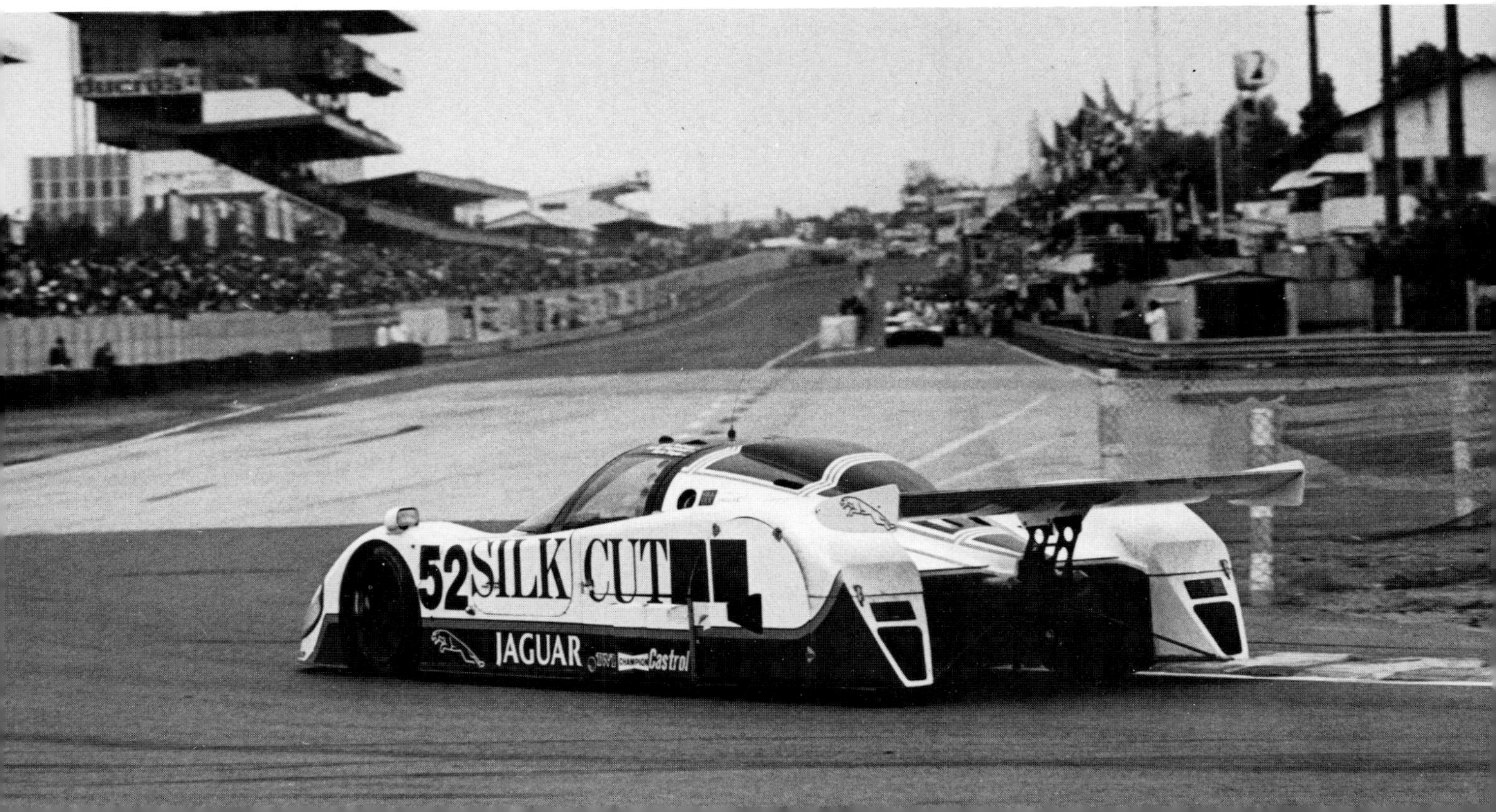

One of the keys to Jaguar's Le Mans reliability in the old days was the retention of an old-fashioned rear axle. The immensely long Mulsanne Straight (along which the XJR-8LM in the lower picture is launching itself) calls for the strongest possible transmission, and one of the keys to that is to minimise the angle of the driveshafts. So many cars break universal joints for this reason, and for 1987 the Jaguars not only had larger, fully lubricated universals but their engines were raised at the rear to reduce the working angle of joints.

A new chicane just before the Dunlop Bridge was well-designed and caused fewer problems than anticipated. The same could be said of the bend in the Mulsanne braking area, first used in 1986. The dangers of Le Mans are the basic ones that have always been there and, it can be argued, are central to the event's unique character: the fastest wooded section from Mulsanne Corner to 'Indianapolis' and, above all the Mulsanne Straight itself. To find a safe viewing niche (and it is not easy) beside the long ribbon of tarmac is to experience that special eeriness: the wail of an engine approaching maximum safe revolutions, and then sustaining them until the source is out of earshot. Some folk say the Mulsanne Straight makes no sense. Others say it is an essential ingredient. Only if there were *NO* Le Mans would an answer be found. In 1988, while Le Mans *was* still around, Jaguar needed to win it just one more time to complete the picture of the marque's great comeback . . . In 1987 it was not to be.

Practice brought a timely reminder of the vagaries of Le Mans when, on the modern, purpose-built stretch (replacing the notorious White House section) the impressive IMSA Porsche driver Price Cobb spun one of the three works 962s on oil and was lucky to step out of the wreck which had caught fire after heavy contact with the barriers. As Hans Stuck had virtually written-off another 962 in Germany a few days earlier, only two works Porsches could take up their starting positions. This they did most effectively with easily the best practice times of 3m.21.09s (Wollek) and 3m.21.12s. (Stuck). The three Jaguars – *inset right* accelerating away from the rolling start – were close together with 3,.24.36s. (Cheever in No. 4). 3m.24.68s. (Brundle in No. 6) and 3m.24.98s. (Lammers in No. 5). Behind them, but ahead of a string of private Porsche 962s, were the French Cougar-Porsche and the two Sauber-Mercedes C9s. Fastest on the straight, the two French WM-Peugeots could not find the pace elsewhere to be competitive and were to be early retirements.

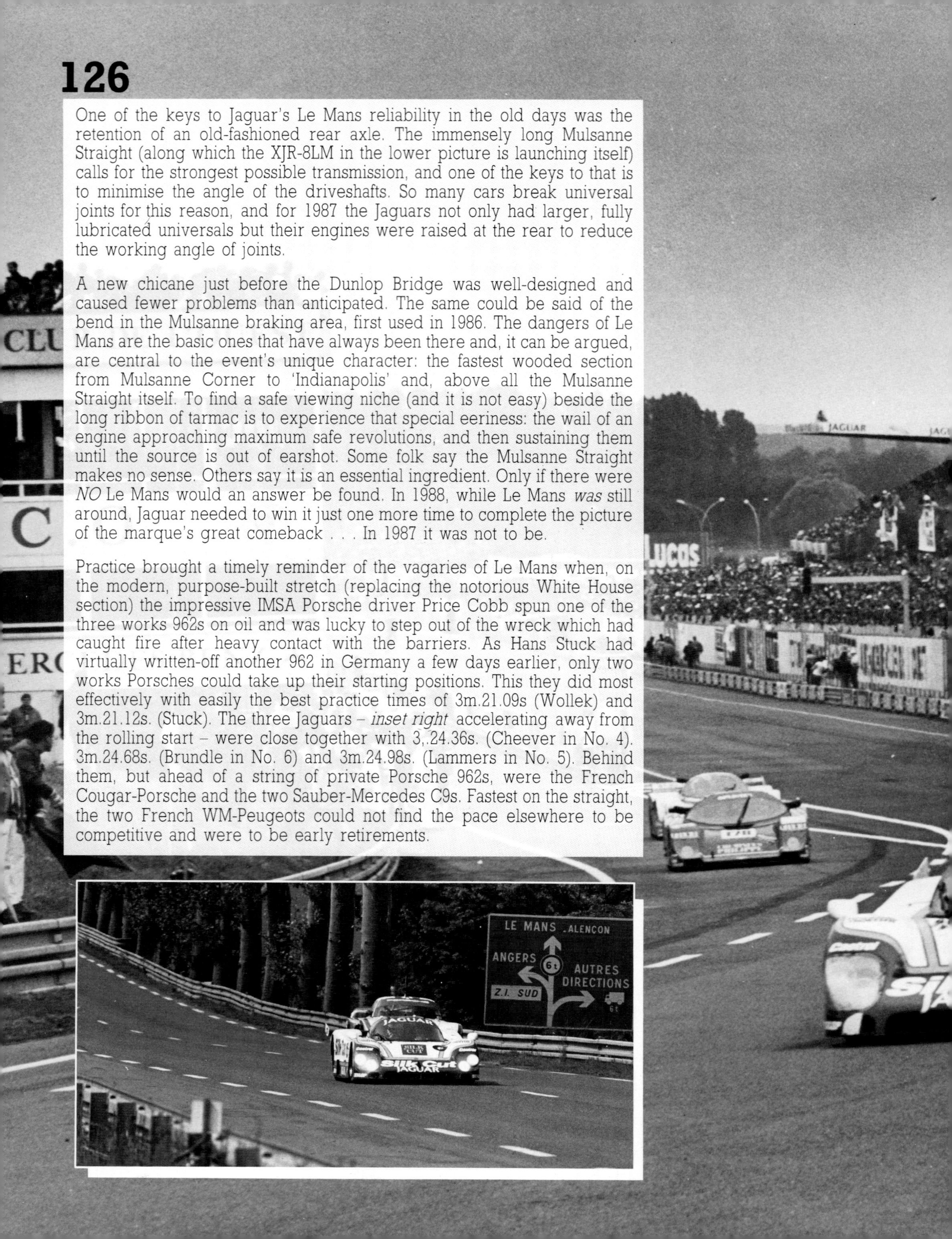

After a miserably rainy morning, the weather remained uncertain at start time, and it was a toss-up whether to fit 'slicks' or 'intermediates'. The uncertainty continued during the early laps, when many drivers changed their minds and stopped for different tyres. Brundle's Jaguar ***(seen here)*** ran third to Stuck and Mass until Lap 17, when the pole-winning Rothmans Porsche (which Mass *should* have been sharing with Wollek and Schuppan) stopped for good with a burned piston – a fate which most of the private Porsches, suffered, too.

Soon the race became a battle between Stuck's Porsche and the three Jaguars, seen here negotiating the new chicane together. For a brief period the Jaguars did hold the three positions, but Porsche No. 17 went ahead regularly when scheduled pit-stops were balanced up.

The weather improved and the circuit dried out completely for a while during the late afternoon which saw a fine battle for the lead between Bell and Nielsen (captured effectively here by John Potter of the *Coventry Evening Telegraph).* As darkness fell, conditions became uncertain again and soon some parts of the track were awash while others seemed only to be brushed by the passing cloudburst. Through much of the night, there was confidence in the TWR pits for, although Bell, Stuck and their American driving partner Al Holbert retained the upper hand, theirs was the only competitive Porsche whereas there were, still, three Jaguars.

WIN PERCY

would like to thank all those involved in any way in ensuring the retention of *all* his faculties.
Tom Walkinshaw, Tony Southgate and the entire TWR crew for designing and building such a strong car; the ACO for erecting three-tier barrier approaching the Mulsanne Kink; the whole pitlane for their concern expressed and the hundreds of people who have telephoned him since the accident.

Then the Mulsanne began to take its toll. First it took the Liqui Moly Porsche, which caught fire inexplicably as James Weaver braked for the right-hand bend; he got out unhurt. Then, just before 3am, Win Percy (co-driver of Jaguar No. 5 with Watson and Lammers) experienced a left rear tyre blow-out at the Mulsanne Kink. The car used the road and the three-tier barrier to dissipate its speed from over 200 mph to zero. It flew upside down (Percy's helmet was marked by the road, after a door had gone) but miraculously the central structure held and – another tribute to Tony Southgate – no fuel cell ruptured. The calm Win Percy spent the rest of the race reassuring everyone he was all right and he is still thanking his lucky stars today. He took a quarter page in that week's *Autosport* (reproduced here). TWR retained the main structure of the car, which was photographed back in the workshop at Kidlington. Much has been written about the race, and this particular incident, but it can do no harm to add the caveat that the effect of a direct impact at such speed would leave very little to the imagination. Le Mans *is* dangerous. In this instance, there was relief in the knowledge that debris, and not the tyre, was blamed for the crash. (The other two cars had switched from Kevlar to nylon tyres – briefly, while that was being checked out – then back again, after the all-clear.)

The long pace-car period (which followed this incident) did much to consolidate the lone Porsche's lead, for any excess fuel consumption while setting the pace early on was now 'saved' by the enforced cruising.

In the sixteenth hour, Nielsen brought in Jaguar No.6 with irreparable cylinder head damage following a valve-spring breakage . . . And then there was one. Jaguar No. 4 had an early morning spin at Arnage (Boesel) but kept its second place until a sequence of problems befell it. The gearbox required rebuilding and patching after an internal breakage; electrical problems caused the car to halt out on the course, as did fuel-feed trouble; and there was another long stop to change a suspension upright. All this dropped the survivors (Cheever, Boesel and – for a late stint – Lammers) down to fifth place. The transmission re-build was the biggest feat: "I've never done a gearbox so quickly," said TWR's Alva Claxton, who – like all in the Silk Cut Jaguar Team – was inspired to achieve the near-impossible by the cheering of thousands of supporters. He and his colleagues – especially Clive Parker, Tim Strudwick, Chris Tuckey, and car-chief Jeff Wilson – were rewarded for their never-give-up attitude by receiving a special trophy for team effort. (The weariness shows in the faces of Tom Walkinshaw, Alastair McQueen, and Allan Scott during one of the last stops – and there, in the background, recalling his concerns of a generation earlier, is the flat-capped figure of 'Lofty' England.)

All credit went to Porsche for calling the tune so successfully at Le Mans. It was the marque's twelfth victory at the Sarthe, and the second in succession for a works car with this trio of drivers. It was Derek Bell's fifth personal success; only Jacky Ickx, no longer racing, was still ahead of him, with six wins.

No. 4 kept going, pounding onto an honourable fifth place – not the result that had been longed for but, in retrospect, pretty good for what was only the second attempt for this particular team; others have taken much longer to win this one, and many more have *never* won it.

The crowds invaded the track, still carrying the banner "Go for it, lads". And for the second year running, with a nod of approval from their subdued masters, back came the message from the worn-out TWR men: "WE WILL BE BACK: THANK YOU AGAIN".

RETRO-SPECTIVE: FRANCE

Jaguar's competition history is centred upon its success at Le Mans in particular – and in France generally. Aside from the 24-hour race, the marque won the 12-hour endurance races at Reims four times and Hyères twice. The longest single high-speed run of all was on the banked Linas-Montlhéry track near Paris in 1952, when this XK120 became the first car ever to exceed a 100 mph average for a whole week.

Three Jaguars were entered privately for the first time at Le Mans in 1950, and two of them completed the 24 hours in mid-field positions. A third XK120 driven by Leslie Johnson and Bert Hadley (seen at 'Indianapolis' with Cadillac *Le Monstre* in tow) was all set to finish among the leaders until the clutch broke in the twenty-second hour.

For 1951, Jaguar produced the XK120C or C-type, specially for Le Mans – and it won on its very first public appearance. Peter Walker (seen right, at the same spot) and Peter Whitehead were victorious.

1953 gave Jaguar a sweeping Le Mans victory against strong opposition, with works C-types coming first, second, and fourth, thanks largely to the use of Dunlop disc brakes. This is what Tertre Rouge looked like in those days. Duncan Hamilton ***(seen left)*** and Tony Rolt were the winners.

The touring car section of the unique *Tour de France Automobile* was an ideal event for Jaguar's compact saloon cars, which won it five times in succession from 1959. It consisted of rally sections, speed hill-climbs, and circuit races. The 1963 winner Bernard Consten is seen at – where else? – Le Mans.

The first great Jaguar era at Le Mans included a hat-trick of victories for the D-type, in 1955, 1956 and 1957. This picture shows the end of the latter race in which five Jaguars had started; they went on to finish first, second, third, fourth and sixth. The two leading cars were entered by *Ecurie Ecosse,* the Edinburgh team which has become famous again in the 1980s, under new management. The full story of Jaguar's early Le Mans participation is told in the two-volume work *Jaguar Sports Racing and Works Competition Cars,* also published by G.T. Foulis & Co. Ltd.

After a twenty-year absence, Jaguar came back to Le Mans in 1984 with two of Group 44's beautifully-prepared XJR-5 IMSA prototypes which showed well but failed to finish.
Group 44 crossed the Atlantic again in 1985 when one XJR-5 was brought to the finish, in thirteenth place, by team boss Bob Tullius *(left)* seen here just before the start with John Egan and Graham Whitehead, head of Jaguar's North American operation. These and two subsequent appearances by the Silk Cut Jaguar Team made Jaguar all the more determined to show it *could* beat the turbocharged German-powered opposition in the French classic in 1988 . . .

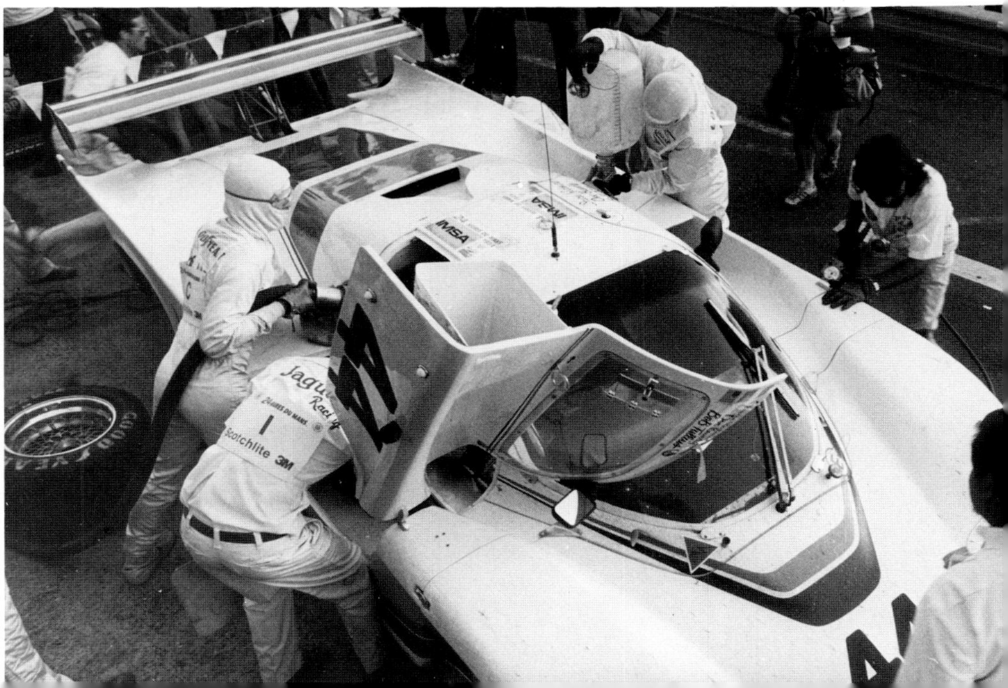

ROUND 6

Norisring: Sprinting Around The Block

Date: 28 June 1987
Venue: Norisring circuit: Nürnberg, Germany
Approx. race distance: 360 km (1 lap = 2.30 km)
Weather: poor in practice, good on race day; hot

Result	Car	Main Sponsor	Team	Drivers	Laps
1st	2.8 Porsche 962 turbo	Liqui Moly	Britten-Lloyd	Baldi/Palmer	154
2nd	2.8 Porsche 962 turbo	Jägermeister	Brun	Larrauri/Mass	151
3rd	2.8 Porsche 962 turbo	Sachs	Joest	'Winter'/Dickens	150
4th	6.9 Jaguar XJR-8	Silk Cut	TWR	Cheever/Boesel	147
5th	2.8 Porsche 962 turbo	Primagaz	Obermaier	Lässig/Yver	146
6th	3.3 Spice-Cosworth	WC	Spice	Velez/Spice	143

A fortnight after Le Mans, and in complete contrast, came the journey to Bavaria for a double sprint around the *Nürnberg Stadion,* scene of annual Nazi rallies under the Hitler regime. There were two 77-lap races, each of 180 km, necessitated by the lack of a proper pit facility. Each lap is short, and there is no rhythm to it; it is a case of point-and-squirt for most drivers; and with three sharp bursts of acceleration every 1.4 miles it is no wonder that, in hot weather, a driver can become ill from the strain and the constant gearchanging. The Norisring is a circuit for the turbocharged cars and the two Jaguars faced not only a dozen of the flat-six Porsches but also two forced-induction V8s in the Sauber-Mercedes C9 and Gianni Mussato's Lancia LC2 – always an immensely fast Group C car in its day, but no longer truly competitive, since the manufacturer was now concentrating on winning back the world rally championship which it had lost to Audi and Peugeot in recent years. Despite the strong opposition, the Jaguars qualified respectably with No.4 in fourth place and No.5 seventh.

Somewhat surprisingly, in view of positive statements to the contrary at Monza, Porsche AG had decided not to take part in the second half of the season's World Championship events, which meant that the regular crews of Bell/Stuck and Mass/Wollek would have to look around. Porsche competitions' chief Peter Falk made it clear that his team was not ducking out of confrontation with Jaguar: it had other commitments and wanted to do justice to them. The best way to keep the Group C action going was (he felt) to concentrate on assisting the main Porsche customer teams. This would include the possibility of offering them the use of 3-litre water-cooled engines (so far reserved for works cars) which were supposedly more powerful than the usual 2.8-litre units with their cylinder blocks air-cooled in the traditional Porsche manner. On reflection, it was not such a blow, as Porsche could certainly be expected to come up with something new again soon: Porsche make no bones about it – they are in racing, come what may, but above all they are there to win. Their approach was, on this occasion, rather reminiscent of Jaguar's in the old days: Coventry would concentrate on Le Mans, win it brilliantly (usually), and *then* look ahead. It is not going too far, to say that Jaguar in the 1950s had a habit of looking at the next Le Mans as soon as Le Mans was over. It was the one that mattered. Here at Nürnberg in 1987, Porsche entered one of its national 'Supercup' cars for its star pair. (The first of the two races was, in fact, a round of the German series.) Pole position went, not unexpectedly, to the popular spectacular German driver, Hans-Joachim Stuck – one of the greatest sports-car drivers of all time.

In the first race, Thackwell in the Sauber-Mercedes was the first to establish a lead. He held it for nearly thirty laps before succumbing to cockpit conditions which prevented him from seeing straight any more, and made him feel faint. Despite the efforts of every team to make its drivers comfortable, it seems this is not always possible; in a game that has become so technological it surprises me (whenever I see a driver get out

of a Group C after a long, hot stint) that cockpit comfort does not seem to have kept pace with other advances such as aerodynamics, handling, braking, or fuel economy. The argument is that top drivers stay in training and accept discomfort. Keeping their cars intact in the initial scramble, Lammers and Cheever established themselves in fourth and fifth places; but Cheever's car needed a new fuel pump regulator, and lost seven laps having one fitted. That might seem a lot, but a quick lap at the Norisring takes less than fifty seconds! The American went on to finish thirteenth in No.4. Meantime, just before half-distance, Lammers had forged ahead in Jaguar No. 5.

On the forty-second lap, Lammers coasted-in with failure of the differential unit: the man who had been quickest in the race-day warm-up session, John Watson, would not be racing today. Giacomelli had fought his way up to ninth before the lone Lancia's engine electronics began to suffer from bad management. So, the race became an inter-Porsche fisticuffs, with Baldi in the Liqui Moly Porsche (***seen here following Cheever)*** winning from Stuck who had become somewhat roused when Larrauri pushed him off in the opening scramble. Unluckier still was Bob Wollek, whose Joest Porsche lost the race within sight of the finish; he had used up too much fuel, duelling with Baldi. (In Germany, cigarette advertising is not allowed – hence the lack of 'Silk Cut' lettering on the XJR-8. The 'Supercup' works Porsche ran in Dunlop/Shell colours.)

Race Two looked like being lucky for the Joest team, with Klaus Ludwig winning comfortably; but then his Porsche (third in Race One in Frank Jelinski's hands) was disqualified because its fuel tank was found to be oversize. You can stretch some of the regulations some of the time; but every so often someone is deemed to have strayed too far out of the grey areas of racing's regulations which are, after all, quite difficult to enforce. So, Raul Boesel became the winner, and this placed Jaguar No.4 fourth on aggregate. ***(He is seen here leading Jochen Mass, who would come third behind Jonathan Palmer.)*** Palmer played safe to give the 'British' Porsche (virtually a new car, following the fire at Le Mans) a well-deserved overall victory. Bell retired with fuel pressure trouble just when the works Porsche looked as though it might have won. Such was the C1 carnage that, once again, the second division battle moved on to the leaderboard with Cosworth-engined Spice and *Ecosse* cars finishing sixth and seventh overall. This season-long battle was to end with another impressive C2 title for Britisher Gordon Spice.

Restrospective

Central Europe has provided Jaguar with a number of successes over the years, especially in touring car racing. In the early 1980s, the TWR Jaguar XJ-S Group A cars won twice at the Oesterreichring (Zeltweg) and twice at the Salzburgring, while Tom Walkinshaw scored a personal hat-trick on the fast Brno road circuit. Earlier, the Jaguar importer for Germany, Peter Lindner, and his co-driver Peter Nöcker took numerous victories in this area, in 3.8-litre E-type and Mark 2 cars. ***This picture*** shows them leading the final race of the original (1963) ETC series – a four-hour event in the city of Budapest, Hungary. Nöcker won it to become the first-ever ETC champion. Soon afterwards, he became the German touring car racing champion, too. In a few years' time, the not-dissimilar Norisring setting may seem as outmoded for racing as these cobbled streets do now.

ROUND 7

Brands Hatch: Jaguar Fights Back

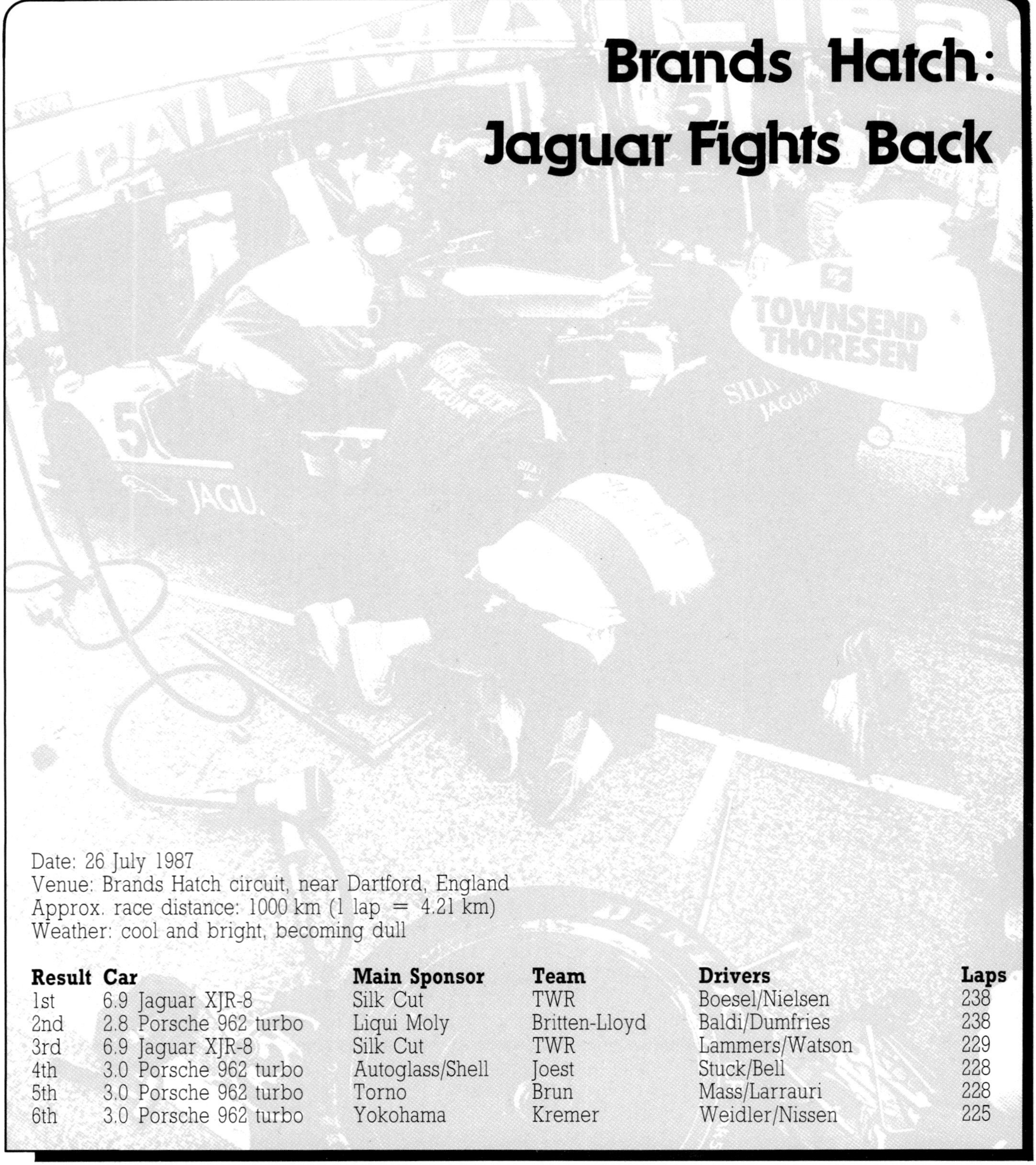

Date: 26 July 1987
Venue: Brands Hatch circuit, near Dartford, England
Approx. race distance: 1000 km (1 lap = 4.21 km)
Weather: cool and bright, becoming dull

Result	Car	Main Sponsor	Team	Drivers	Laps
1st	6.9 Jaguar XJR-8	Silk Cut	TWR	Boesel/Nielsen	238
2nd	2.8 Porsche 962 turbo	Liqui Moly	Britten-Lloyd	Baldi/Dumfries	238
3rd	6.9 Jaguar XJR-8	Silk Cut	TWR	Lammers/Watson	229
4th	3.0 Porsche 962 turbo	Autoglass/Shell	Joest	Stuck/Bell	228
5th	3.0 Porsche 962 turbo	Torno	Brun	Mass/Larrauri	228
6th	3.0 Porsche 962 turbo	Yokohama	Kremer	Weidler/Nissen	225

Brands Hatch in the chalky downs of Kent has been developed over the years since it was first tarmacked for anticlockwise racing in 1950. It is noted for its viewing facilities and for a particularly exciting first turn – Paddock Hill Bend – which falls away dauntingly. The corner has more than one apex and more than one racing line through it; it has seen many a brave manoeuvre, and the 1987 1000 km race (backed, like the Silverstone race, by the Shell Gemini oil brand) would be no exception. Star of practice and the race was the diminuitive Dutchman Jan Lammers (***seen in the pits*** with his co-driver John Watson and XJR-8 designer Tony Southgate). His qualifying time of 1m.14.44s., representing 126.39 mph, was quicker than any Group C car ever – quicker even, than Ricardo Patrese's boosted benchmark of 1985 with the Lancia LC2.

The Silk Cut Jaguar Team had much to prove today, for although it had won four of the first six rounds, Derek Bell and Hans Stuck still led the Driver's Championship. Besides this, the XJR-6s had not won this event in 1985 or 1986; and to win it was no easy task, for although some of the usual 962s were missing, three of the private Porsches were to race with 3-litre factory engines. However, Raul Boesel made sure that No.4 was alongside No.5 to make it a Jaguar front row for the home crowd. Fresh from its Bavarian victory the Britten-Lloyd car was by far the most impressive Porsche, with new features to add downforce but without the proffered works engine, team boss Richard Lloyd and manager David Price preferring their own air-cooled 2.8-litre unit. While the three potential winners were down near the 850 kg weight limit, old dogs Bell and Stuck showed there was plenty of life in them yet by qualifying their Joest

Porsche fourth – and quicker than their 1986 'pole' time despite a car that had weighed-in at over 900 kg. From the start Lammers shot ahead, delighting in the car and the circuit – for him, an ideal combination.

Boesel was beaten away from the line by Baldi and Stuck. He overtook the German on Lap 2 but the Italian presented more of a problem. By Lap 14 Boesel was becoming impatient with the sight of the Liqui Moly Porsche tantalisingly using the bit of road he wanted, so he tried to get below Baldi on the swoop into Paddock Hill. It was a bit much to expect Baldi to leave a space and the Jaguar, braking sharply now, touched the Porsche as it came across to use the inside line. The Jaguar came off worst, as Jaguar Deutschland's photographer proved. Unlike Monza, Brands Hatch did not trap Boesel in the sand for good, but No.4 did lose over a lap acquiring a new tail (as well as fuel and tyres) after this.

No.5 maintained a comfortable advantage but, soon after half-distance (and immediately after a long period behind the pace car while a crashed car was being removed), Watson felt a rear end tremor which wouldn't go away even when his tyres were changed. A second pit-call revealed that the nearside rear wheel bearing had failed. Replacement of the whole hub assembly took nearly as long as ten racing laps.

(Inset right) Coming up behind Baldi for the second time in the race Boese remained more circumspect than before, but both drivers were working hard.

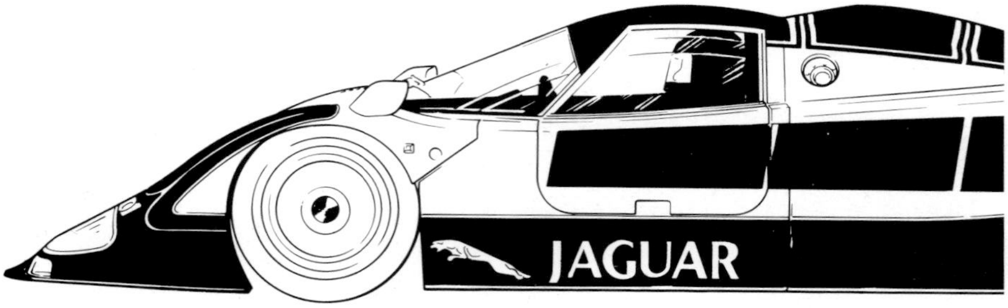

The duel of the day was holding everyone's attention, and in the press room it was almost as fascinating to watch the leaderboard as it was to cast an eye towards the track itself. Unlike the drivers, the serious reporters had no-one to relieve them! Mike Cotton *(Motoring News* and *Motor Sport)* and Quentin Spurring *(Autosport)* keep up the concentration as the story unfolds.

The moment of truth: Johnny Dumfries heads for his pit on Lap 168 and John Nielsen takes the lead in No.4 – never to lose it. (Dumfries and Nielsen were substituting for Palmer and Cheever respectively as the race clashed with the German Grand Prix.)

Towards the end, Watson survived a savaging from Baldi as No.5 charged through the field. Lights ablaze, Lammers took the lap record (1m.16.44s.) and he and Watson were rewarded with third place, catching Stuck and Bell who lost time in the pits due to a seat-belt mix-up *and* on the circuit due to lack of power and a detached anti-roll bar – frustrating for the former title-holders who were about to lose their championship lead.

The last few laps saw the BLR Porsche assault finally collapse as quick lappery pushed fuel consumption beyond danger level. It slowed to complete the full distance just seventy-three seconds behind the winning Jaguar after over five and a half hours of racing. It was a day of triumph for the whole Silk Cut Jaguar Team – especially for John Nielsen (*left*) who had never driven at Brands Hatch before, and for Raul Boesel who had vindicated himself in Tom Walkinshaw's eyes to move ahead on the championship progress chart, with 90 points to the 84 of Bell/Stuck. Boesel's absent partner Cheever was next with 70, followed by Lammers and Watson with 67. The Teams' Championship was as good as wrapped up now, Silk Cut Jaguar having scored 118 points to Porsche's 74 which had remained static since Le Mans.

Retrospective: 1987's revenge was sweet, for BLR's Liqui Moly Porsche driven by Wollek and Barilla had won at Brands Hatch in 1986 when this picture was taken as it followed the Cheever/Brancatelli XJR-6 through Paddock Hill Bend. (This Jaguar finished sixth, and that of Warwick/Schlesser fourth, both slowed by niggling problems.)

It was at Brands Hatch that the XJR-6 had made its UK race début in its Castrol/Dunlop/Jaguar green-and-white livery, back in 1985 when both cars had showed the fans their potential but neither had managed to reach the finish.

ROUND 8

Nürburgring: Silk Cut Jaguar Wins Team Title

Date: 30 August 1987
Venue: Neue Nürburgring circuit, near Koblenz, Germany
Approx. race distance: 1000 km (1 lap = 4.54 km)
Weather: variable in practice, sunny for race

Result	Car	Main Sponsor	Team	Drivers	Laps
1st	6.9 Jaguar XJR-8	Silk Cut	TWR	Cheever/Boesel	221
2nd	3.0 Porsche 962 turbo	R'mans/Autoglass	Joest	Stuck/Bell	218
3rd	3.0 Porsche 962 turbo	Lui/Eterna	Brun	Mass/Larrauri	216
4th	2.8 Porsche 962 turbo	Taka-Q	Joest	Jelinski/Dickens/'Winter'	212
5th	2.8 Porsche 962 turbo	Liqui Moly	Britten-Lloyd	Baldi/Palmer	211
6th	2.8 Porsche 962 turbo	JSK Construction	Brun	Pareja/Kaufmann/Hunkeler	208

The Sauber-Mercedes team sponsored by Yves St Laurent (Kouros) returned to the scene of their victory with two cars. In 1986, there had been an enormous accident in the rain – fortunately without any serious personal consequences – because of a badly organised pace-car incident. The restart had provided the V8 Mercedes-engined Swiss Sauber with its first victory – but only after the leading XJR-6 of Warwick and Lammers had had to retire when a broken pipe starved a camshaft of lubricant, causing engine seizure. Unfortunately, this time, Johnny Dumfries tangled with a slow car and damaged one C9 sufficiently to prevent its starting. So Dumfries joined 1986 winners Pescarolo and Thackwell in car No.61, the latter being third fastest in practice behind Baldi in the 'British' Porsche and Cheever in Jaguar No.4 ***(here leading the Sauber),*** with Lammers occupying the second row alongside Thackwell.

While the Bell/Stuck Joest Porsche was reluctant to start, and had to join the back of the grid instead of Row Three, the fastest five cruised round on their parade lap in their practice order: Baldi (Porsche), Cheever and Lammers (Jaguars), Thackwell (Sauber-Mercedes) and Ludwig (Joest Blaupunkt Porsche).

At the start-proper, Baldi lost boost pressure when he tried to accelerate, and could not control the field's approach to the starter's red light. Cheever kept accelerating, believing (once he realised the poleman was in trouble) that the race would be restarted. Instead he got a green light just as he was backing-off! So, not only did Cheever lose his advantage – he was penalised one minute and fined five thousand dollars. Klaus Ludwig and Mike Thackwell took advantage of the situation to run first and second. Lammers and Cheever stayed close, in third and fourth places, followed for the first few laps by Jochen Mass (Brun Porsche) and Jochen Dauer (Victor Porsche).

Lammers began to slow with a rough-sounding engine; after 28 laps he stopped and, without more ado, No.5 was pushed away with irreparable damage caused by a broken valve spring. Once more, Watson was deprived of a drive but, meantime, Cheever and Boesel were moving up to overcome their one-minute penalty. Unlike its forerunner, the *Neue Nürburgring* is a 'technical' circuit rather than a 'natural' one. It has wide open spaces ***(as this picture illustrates clearly)*** but few natural overtaking points. The drivers may not like it much, but they do seem to be getting used to it.

Shell mit M 2000
ADAC
61
BLAUPUNKT
VICTOR
JAGUAR
5
4
LIQUI MOLY
LM
GOODYEAR
Castrol
Agip
UNIROYAL

Just after half-distance, the excellent showing by Ludwig and Wollek came to an end with an internal gearbox failure for the Blaupunkt-Joest Porsche. By this time, the surviving Jaguar was containing the Sauber, which had gone quick enough to make best race-lap time (Thackwell) but which was about to retire, primarily through a shortage of gears. Most remaining Porsches were in trouble, chiefly with fuel consumption, while Eddie Cheever ***(seen here in close-up)*** led serenely.

The cunning Bell and Stuck never give up, and once again their policy paid off. Their Joest Porsche for which Rothmans had provided some sponsorship – though, like the Jaguars, their car could not display their sponsors' brand-names without defying German laws – picked its way through from its bad start and took second place when Mass ran short of brakes. Baldi and Palmer would have recovered better than they did from their bad start, but for the need to conserve their fuel ration. Of the C1 cars only the Jaguar ***(seen here taking the chequered flag)*** was on top of the situation.

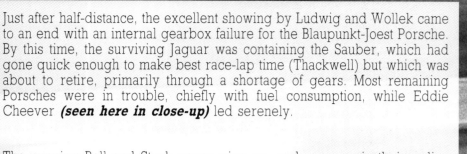

TWR Jaguar race director Roger Silman had reason to be jubilant at the Nürburgring for he knew that the team championship had been won; not even the Brun team, the reigning title holders, could overtake the Silk Cut Jaguars now. Here he shares the magic moment with Raul Boesel, whose lead over Bell and Stuck in the drivers' table was now looking strong, as he had four wins to their one – though he still needed to consolidate his position.

Eddie Cheever did not look too happy as Tom Walkinshaw held his post-race press briefing. Cheever's expression would change a little later, however, when he was told that his second fine of the year would be waived.

Immediately afterwards, as if by magic, the team donned new tee-shirts emblazoned 'TWR–WORLD CHAMPS '87' and posed appropriately with the Jaguar pace car. On the left are John Watson and John Nielsen (neither of whom got a drive in Germany); on the right is Jan Lammers. Tom Walkinshaw, with trophy is flanked by Eddie Cheever and Raul Boesel.

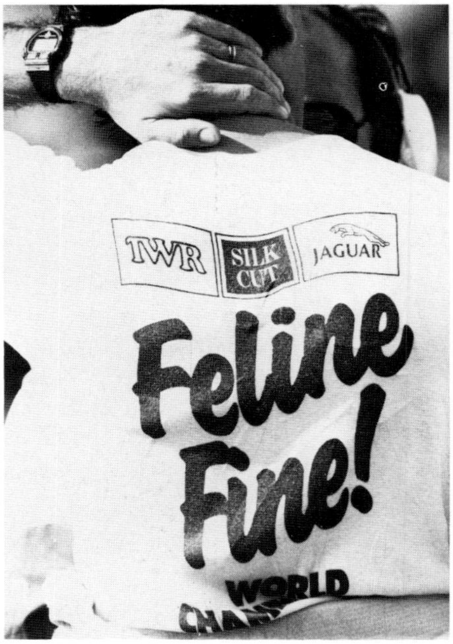

It was the slogan on the back of the champions' tee-shirts that caught the eye: surely a pun from *Autosport's* 'Sportscard' headline writer? Well anyway, *Autosport* did use it four days later.

Retrospective

It would be wrong to leave the Nürburgring without mentioning the old circuit and past glories. More than twenty kilometres per lap, with every kind of gradient and bend, the *Nordschleife* was last used for international racing in 1983. In 1982, a TWR Jaguar XJ-S had made its mark by winning an ETC race there with Walkinshaw beating all the BMW men including Stuck himself.

A C-type Jaguar came second in this circuit's first-ever WSC round, in 1953; but Jaguar's greatest period here was in the early nineteen-sixties when Wiesbaden-based importer Peter Lindner was responsible for Jaguar winning five major touring car events, each of six or twelve hours' duration. Often the classes would be sent off at intervals, to reduce the chance of bunching. After all, there was plenty of room for a large field as long as it was well spread out. ***This picture*** was taken at the start of the 1963 six-hour race, which was also the first round of the original European Touring Challenge. The Volvos are held back as the Alfas, Jaguars, Lancias, and Mercedes are unleashed. As expected, it was to be a battle between the Mercedes-Benz 300SEL of Eugen Böhringer/Dieter Glemser and the 3.8-litre Jaguar of Peter Lindner/Peter Nöcker – and the latter pair won. Nöcker went on to become the first ETC champion. Jaguar prepared Lindner's cars in the first place, but his own company maintained and

financed them for racing thereafter.

No excuse is made for reminding the reader of Jaguar's past racing achievements. As Sir John Egan has said: "The association of the Jaguar name with motor racing is deep rooted." Whatever happens in the motor racing of the future, nothing can take away Jaguar's first World Championship. As with its successes in former times, Jaguar's results of the 1980s – and 1987 in particular – are now banked for posterity: another bit of long-term investment in the goodwill that has made Jaguar one of Britain's industrial survivors.

ROUND 9

Spa-Francorchamps: The Three Musketeers - All For Raul

Date: 13 September 1987
Venue: Francorchamps circuit, near Spa (Ardennes), Belgium
Approx. race distance: 985 km (1 lap = 6.94 km)
Weather: dull, then drizzle and rain (causing 1000 km race to be halted at six hours according to rules)

Result	**Car**	**Main Sponsor**	**Team**	**Drivers**	**Laps**
1st	6.9 Jaguar XJR-8	Silk Cut	TWR	Brundle/Dumfries/Boesel	142*
2nd	6.9 Jaguar XJR-8	Silk Cut	TWR	Lammers/Watson	141
3rd	3.0 Porsche 962 turbo	FAT	Brun	Mass/Larrauri	140
4th	6.9 Jaguar XJR-8	Silk Cut	TWR	Cheever/Nielsen	140
5th	3.0 Porsche 962 turbo	Rothmans	Joest	Stuck/Bell	139
6th	2.8 Porsche 962 turbo	Blaupunkt	Joest	Jelinski/'Winter'/Dickens	138

(145 laps originally scheduled)*

There is no international racing track quite like this one – not any more, now that the old Brno and Nürburgring circuits have gone.

It is scenic and it has every kind of bend and gradient. Part of its uniqueness is that its most spectacular section – the swoop down past the old pit lane (still used for the 1000 km race but not for the Belgian GP) to *l'Eau Rouge*, then sharply uphill to *Le Raidillon* – is in full view of pit crews. Cars on the racing line rattle the signallers' barrier, and messages must be held high: John Nielsen demolished part of his XJR-8's rear wing against his own pit-signal during the 1987 race. When the circuit underwent major surgery some years ago, it did not have to lose its character. The fastest and most dangerous bits *(Burnenville – Masta – Stavelot)* were replaced by a purpose-built section which dives from the highest point on the circuit through a cutting and a series of medium-speed curves. The original road circuit is rejoined for the last of the gradual climb to *La Source* – the slow hairpin at the edge of Francorchamps village ***(top right of this picture)*** from which the plunge into another exciting lap is taken.

The only unnatural looking section is the so-called bus-stop, where cars are slowed before the long left-hander that leads to *La Source*. The fastest of the Porsches (fitted, as in Germany a fortnight earlier, with Southgate-style rear wheel spats) is shown getting back on line after the bus-stop deviation and . . .

. . . diving into the hairpin ahead of one of the Jaguars. If cars turned left here they would find themselves in Francorchamps village and, several kilometres further on, in the quiet, pleasantly unfashionable resort town of Spa itself where, a week before the race, the peace was shattered by an impromptu demonstration from Jan Lammers in the XJR-8.

Chris Tuckey of the TWR team took this atmospheric picture, which gives the impression of a modern car taking part in a latterday Targa Florio-style road race. Even hardened professionals from the Silk Cut Jaguar Team found their adrenalin coursing that day . . .

Jonathan Palmer was fastest on the Saturday morning, the Liqui Moly Porsche now, at last, going well with the 3-litre works engine (on race boost) to become the first sports car to exceed an average of 200 km/h – although (Palmer said) he could have done better than 2m.04.11s. if he had not had to switch fuel tanks during that clear run. This race was sponsored by Kouros and it marked the fifth and final WSC appearance of the magnificent Sauber-Mercedes C9 – a great opportunity to show its paces and give its sponsors concrete return on their investment. Yet only one car was to race. Third to Palmer and Lammers in the morning session, driven by Jean-Louis Schlesser, the C9 flew round at the very end of Saturday afternoon's session with Thackwell at the wheel to take pole position in 2m.04.04s. (201.419 km/h), to put the Jaguars of Lammers and Cheever on the second row. This was the crucial race for Jaguar: a one-for-all-and-all-for-one occasion. Perhaps Peter Sauber should have taken a leaf out of Tom Walkinshaw's book? Perhaps it was all to do with having – or not having – the funds when they were needed? Back in 1983, Walkinshaw had found two cars inadequate to make him a champion; so in 1984 he used sledgehammer tactics and with three XJ-Ss at his disposal, he had become European champion. Three years later, there was an element of the same when it mattered most – when TWR brought three cars and seven drivers to Spa. There were the four regulars, plus Martin Brundle (Jaguar needed him; but he needed Jaguar to boost his morale) and John Nielsen, the stand-in driver who always came up trumps, as at Brands Hatch. Seventh man was Johnny Dumfries, seen here with Paul Davis *(left),* while Tony Dowe on the extreme *right* talks for Ian Reed. Dowe is in charge of the 1988 Jaguar Castrol IMSA challenge, with Reed as his chief engineer. They managed Car No. 6 at Spa-Francorchamps as a kind of getting-to-know-you exercise with TWR.

Why the seventh man? Well, the World Championship regulations stated that a driver must take the wheel for thirty percent of any race, that the best seven race scores were to count. Raul Boesel had now scored seven times, but if he could drop his Le Mans score (eight points for fifth place) and add twenty points to his total, neither Derek Bell nor Hans Stuck could catch him again. So all Tom Walkinshaw ***(seen in the Spa pit-lane with Guy Edwards)*** had to do was to enter three cars for six drivers, and nominate Boesel for all three. How could he fail?

The only risk was lack of practice for the newcomers. First of all, on Friday, Martin Brundle (forgetting that ground-hugging bodywork doesn't like high kerbs) put No.6 into the barriers down in the valley. That meant new rear suspension, radiator and other oddments at both ends. Then on Saturday morning, Johnny Dumfries did a more complete job when he forgot about the bus-stop for a moment. Over the kerbs bounced No.6 Jaguar, again, spoiling the new nose, the new radiator, the suspension, the steering rack mounting and more . . . Fortunately, there were sufficient parts to replace the damaged ones.

The sixth-on-grid practice time by Brundle, just before handing over the car to Dumfries, was not beaten on Saturday afternoon which Mickey Buskel, Gary Davies and other members of the TWR team spent putting No.6 back together again for the second time in one weekend. Raul Boesel did the necessary qualifying laps, however. All *he* had to do now was to get into the right car at the right moment and do thirty percent of the race.

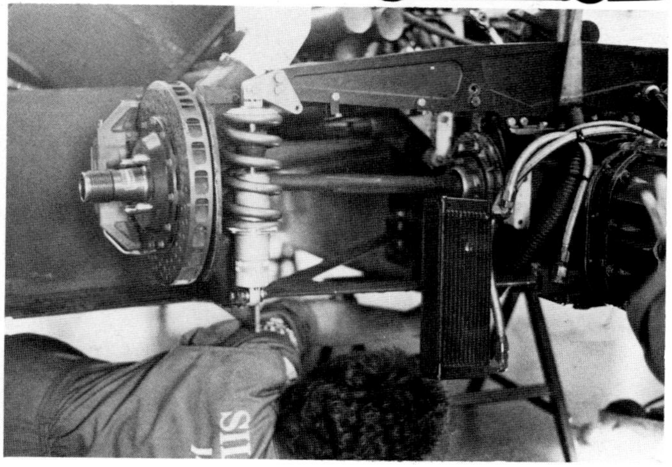

For the last 1987 European Group C world championship race there was a full Jaguar commercial turnout, including Sir John Egan and his sales and marketing director Roger Putnam (Neil Johnson's ex-Lotus successor) who could have made Tom Walkinshaw smile almost any time in 1987 – but especially today.

It was a big day for everyone . . . designer Tony Southgate *(left)* and Jaguar racing manager Ron Elkins . . . Charlie Bamber and his boss, TWR's Kiwi engine development king Allan Scott *(right)*.

On the grid at Spa, too, were Jaguar's own media men Ian Norris, David Boole, and *(left)* Mike Cook – the Canadian in charge of Jaguar's US product public relations. (Norris was seconded to New Jersey in 1988 when TWR would be racing for Jaguar Cars Inc. in the IMSA GTP North American race series).

To be a chief racing engineer you need to be cool, and they don't come much cooler than the men in charge of the regular 1987 Jaguar team cars, Alastair McQueen (No.4) and Eddie Hinckley (No.5), or TWR's general racing manager, Paul Davis, for that matter.

Spa was a battle of the tobacco companies. Pareja and Schäfer were sponsored by Fortuna in their Brun Porsche; the Joest Porsche for Bell and Stuck (seen against a competitive background) was backed by Rothmans to keep their title hopes alive; and once again the Jaguars could don the full Silk Cut livery which had enabled TWR to have a proper racing budget.

It was dry but threatening as the race got under way, the Palmer taking the initial advantage; but Mike Thackwell swept ahead to lead for four laps. Then he brought the Sauber into the pits and Palmer went in front again. Sparks flying and lights blazing, Palmer began to catch the tail-enders, maintaining a confident lead in the Liqui Moly car.

Meanwhile, Mike Thackwell (here blasting away from the pits for the first time) had to make a second stop, to complete the job of fixing a loose seat. He went on to make fastest lap and finish seventh overall, with Schlesser's help. They *could* have given the Jaguars a run for their money but for this problem and a slight misfire which was to develop later, for it was said that the Mercedes engine's fuel consumption was much improved.

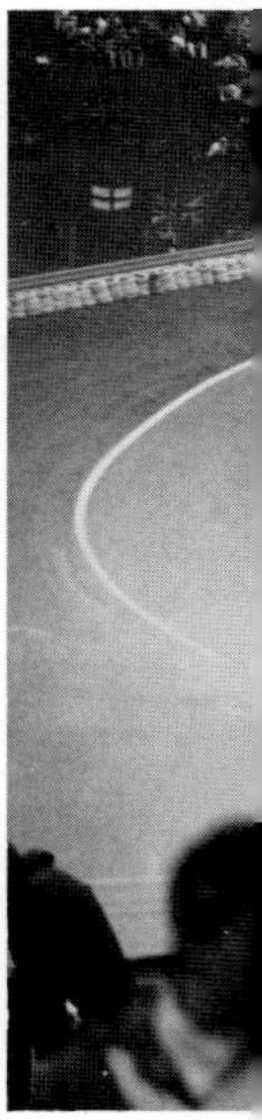

Eddie Cheever kept Palmer in sight up front, while Lammers, Brundle and Jelinski *(shown here)* occupied third, fourth and fifth places. Then Cheever's car started to run rough after twenty laps *and* use too much fuel; a short-circuit had caused car No.4 to run rich on one bank, and two laps were lost resolving this.

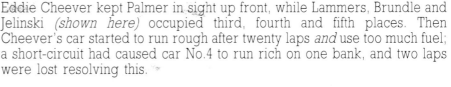

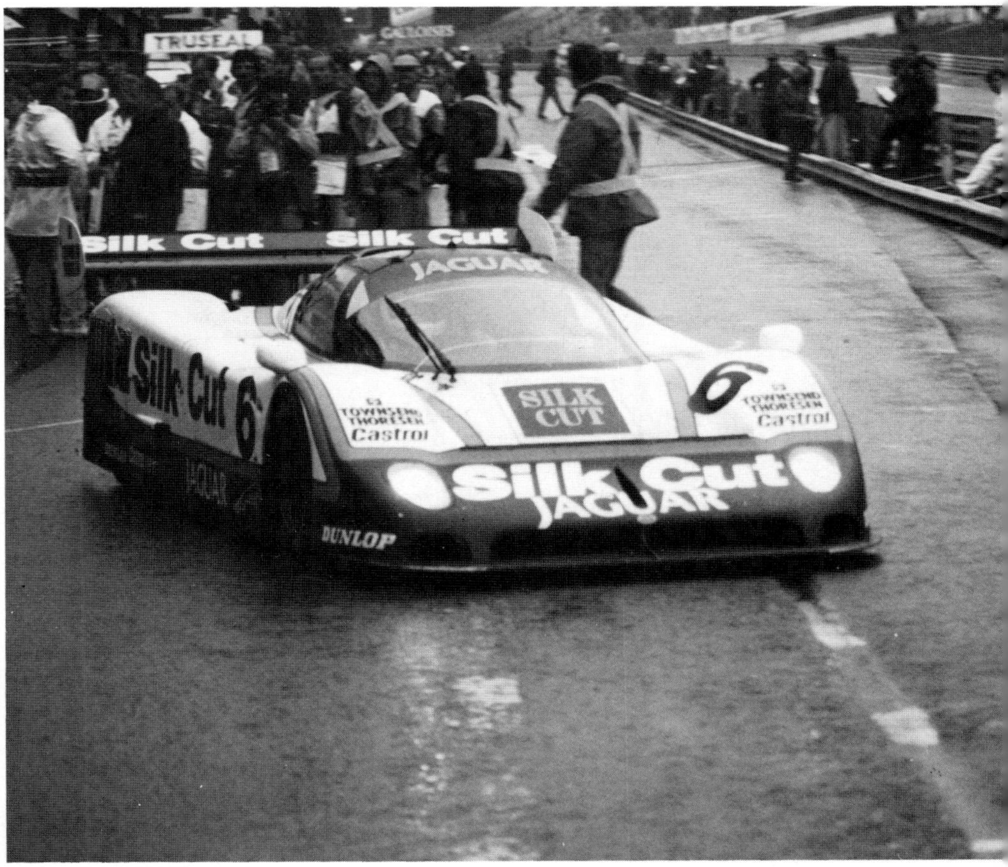

At an early stage it began to drizzle; soon this became rain. It varied between the two for the rest of the race, and the circuit would never dry out again completely. Baldi and Palmer lost all the advantage they had gained early on, Goodyear providing an inadequate choice of Group C tyre specifications – nothing 'in the middle' – so the Britten-Lloyd Porsche faded from contention, ultimately to retire, dampness and differential being blamed vaguely for the car's deteriorating behaviour. The Lammers/Watson Jaguar (No.5) had handling problems, too, but these were cured to some extent by wing adjustments. Meanwhile Brundle and Dumfries had more than made up for their practice indiscretions and, with some fortuitous tyre choices at moments when conditions were altering, established a strong lead by half-distance – strong enough for the twice-rebuilt car to be selected as the one for Boesel to drive.

Although conditions improved slightly, the spray still hung over the circuit.

Raul Boesel put in the best part of an hour and a half at the wheel, maintaining the lead throughout. Then it was left to Martin Brundle to see No.6 through to the chequered flag. While Watson consolidated second place, Cheever skimmed onwards and upwards on his chosen slick tyres and looked as though he *might* take third place . . . but time was running out. 145 laps were needed for the full 1000 km. At six hours, when the chequered flag had to be waved, Brundle was still three laps short; but Cheever's fourth place was to prove well worth having in the long run.

As the last few minutes ran out, Raul Boesel watched the circuit and the computer screen tensely. Finally, however, he could relax – as World Champion.

Retrospective: The 1987 victory for the Silk Cut Jaguar Team at Spa-Francorchamps was as important as any in Jaguar's history – but there had been a comparable one in 1984 when Tom Walkinshaw, Hans Heyer and Win Percy *(seen here)* broke BMW's domination of the world's only international 24-hour race for touring cars, virtually clinching the European Group A title for Walkinshaw.

There have been several victories for works Jaguars at Spa over the years, including this one by Johnny Claes in 1951, driving the XK120 (usually registered HKV 500) with which he would also win that year's Liège-Rome-Liège high-speed rally.

Jaguar people made regular visits to Belgium in the early post-war years, when one side of the Ostend-Brussels *autoroute* would be closed for timed speed tests. The 2-litre four-cylinder XK-engined Gardner Special – tended by Walter Hassan – achieved over 175 mph in 1948 and on this stretch of road Norman Dewis took the experimental 'Jaguar XK120C Mk II' *(here)* up to 180 mph in 1953.

ROUND 10

Fuji:
Clean Sweep For Jaguar

Date: 27 September 1987
Venue: Fuji circuit, Gotemba City, near Yokohama, Japan
Approx. race distance: 1000 km (1 lap = 4.46 km)
Weather: wet for much of practice, dry on race day

Result	Car	Main Sponsor	Team	Drivers	Laps
1st	6.9 Jaguar XJR-8	Silk Cut	TWR	Lammers/Watson	224
2nd	6.9 Jaguar XJR-8	Silk Cut	TWR	Boesel/Dumfries	224
3rd	3.0 Porsche 962 turbo	Matsuda	Britten-Lloyd	Baldi/Thackwell	221
4th	3.0 Porsche 962 turbo	Takefuji	Brun	Mass/Larrauri	218
5th	2.8 Porsche 962 turbo	Taka-Q	Joest	Jelinski/Dickens/'Winter'	218
6th	3.0 Porsche 962 turbo	Rothmans	Schuppan	Bell/Brabham	218

Except at Le Mans, little is seen of the potential Group C opposition from Japan. At Fuji for the final round of the 1987 World Sportscar Championship, it made its presence felt, if only briefly. (It *had* been planned to hold a second race, of sprint 'dimensions', at Sendai; but that circuit did not meet the required standards, angered teams and sponsors being told this only after they had arrived in Japan.) At Fuji, two Jaguars and twelve Porsche 962Cs faced three Nissans and two Toyotas, all turbocharged and vying for grid honours on limitless supplies of qualifying tyres. There were three GTP Mazda rotaries, too, one of them finishing seventh in the race, ahead of the C2 runners. With Sauber's season at an end, there were some driver switchings, Thackwell joining the 'British' Porsche team in place of Palmer who was at the Spanish GP – as was Cheever, whose seat in Jaguar No.4 would be taken by Dumfries. John Nielsen was to drive a Japanese-entered Porsche 962 (finishing ninth).

Fastest of all in practice was the Nissan No.26 driven by Takao Wada, but Geoff Lees was very close in the Minolta-backed Toyota No.36. On the second row was the Dome Toyota of Cheever Minor with Baldi in the quickest Porsche alongside. Lammers and Boesel were fifth and tenth fastest, the difference being explained by traffic. Hans Stuck and Derek Bell had been due to split forces for Japan and in the end Stuck stayed at home. Neither he nor Bell could improve on their position in the championship unless they finished first or second. Bell took Rothmans sponsorship with him to drive with Geoff Brabham in a familiar Porsche – the ex-works Le Mans winner, now owned by the Australian Vern Schuppan, which Bell qualified fourteenth.

The Jaguar team was controlled, as usual, by Roger Silman; and this time he was on his own, in that Tom Walkinshaw was absent – on business in America . . . or was it Australia? A few years ago it would have been difficult to imagine a TWR team racing without TW. The pace of the Japanese cars did not bother Silman, who was happy to let them rush away at the start if they could.

Wada led Lees briefly, but then Lammers swept past both of them. The Nissan dropped back and went out of contention altogether later on, when Wada's co-driver Anders Olofsson was involved in a minor accident and repair work put the Japanese car down to an eventual thirteenth. Meanwhile Lees passed Lammers to put the Toyota in front from Lap 7 to Lap 35. In the second driving spell, Alan Jones, who had taken over the Toyota, passed Watson after a pace car period; but before half-time the Toyota's engine failed when third man Masamori Sekiya was at the wheel. The other two Toyotas had blown up earlier. The Japanese cars had added a new element to Group C racing; Wada (3-litre Nissan 86G turbo) and Geoff Lees (2-litre Toyota 87C turbo) are shown here.

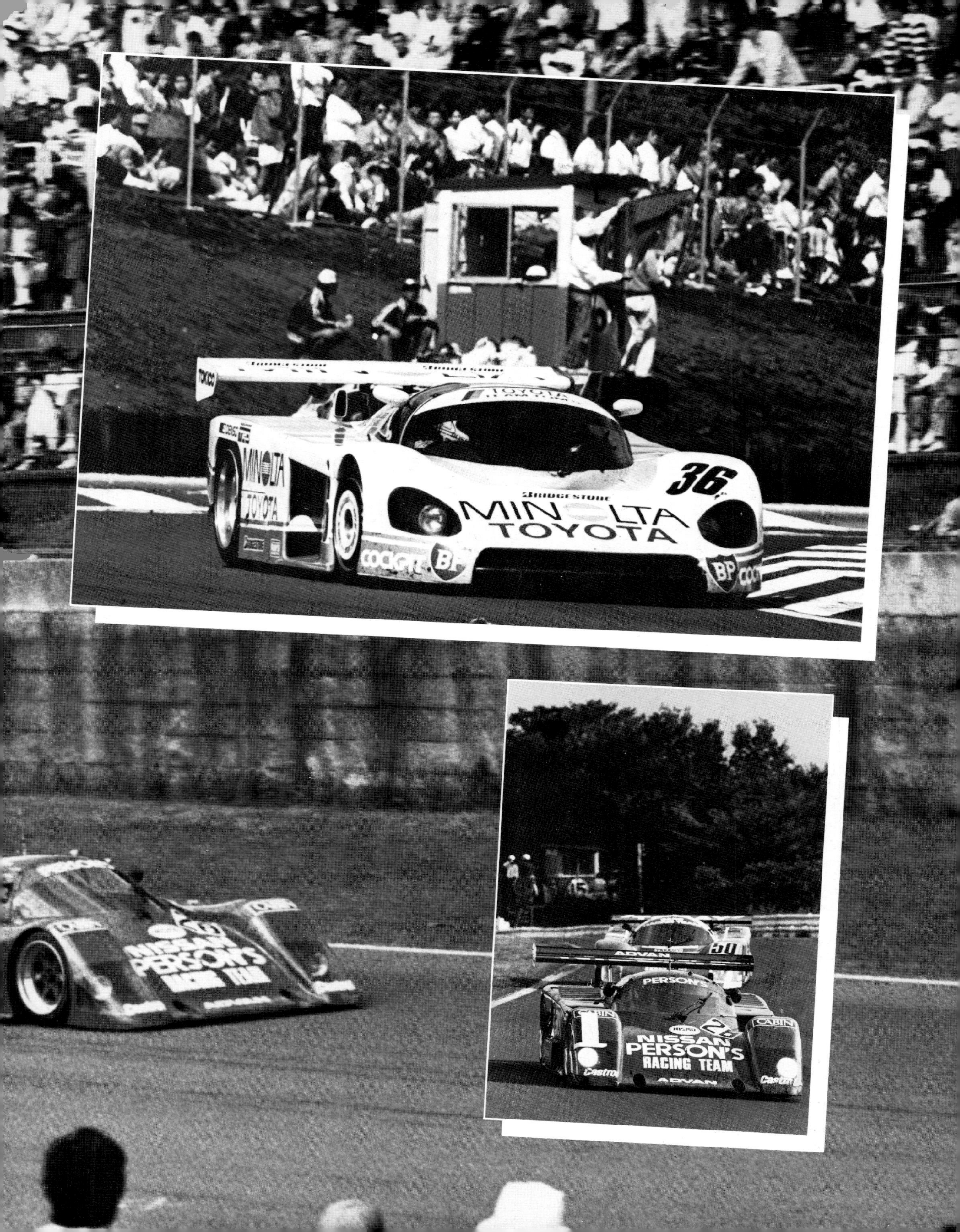
NISSAN
PERSON'S
RACING TEAM
TOKICO
36
BRIDGESTONE
MINOLTA
TOYOTA
COCKPIT
BP
50
ADVAN
PERSON'S
CABIN
NISSAN
PERSON'S
RACING TEAM
Castrol
ADVAN

From the third hour, the Jaguars were in complete command, although the rate turbocharged cars were using fuel there had been little doubt at any stage that the Kidlington team ought to be able to continue its winning streak. Here Kevin Lee and Eddie Hinckley supervise a routine Lammers/Watson pit-stop.

Jaguar No.4 was driven by Boesel and Dumfries in Japan and, after shaking off Baldi's Porsche, this car maintained a steady second position on the same lap as its team mate. Here it leads the Kremer Porsche of Konrad/Fouche and the GTP Mazda of Yorino/Kennedy.

Defending champion Derek Bell worked as hard as ever at Fuji but his hard-earned sixth place was too little and too late. Of all the Porsche regulars, only he and Stuck (absent on this occasion) proved capable of putting up a consistent fight against the Jaguar drivers in 1987 – a fight they continued bravely after Porsche AG had withdrawn its own race team in mid season.

As the race approached its end, it was realised – wasn't it? – that by keeping the cars in their present order, Lammers and Watson would leapfrog Bell and Stuck to become joint runners-up in the Drivers' Championship. Watching the monitor with Roger Silman and Ron Elkins, Raul Boesel didn't mind: He was champion already.

SILK CUT
JAGUAR
Cut
TOWNSEND
THORESEN
Castrol
PUMPS
ON
Silk Cut Silk Cut
TOWNSEND
THORESEN
JAGUAR
Silk Cut
4
SILK
CUT
TOWNSEND
THORESEN
Castrol
Silk Cut
JAGUAR
DUNLOP

Lammers and Watson made a fine partnership in car No.5 throughout 1987, taking their third victory at Fuji and consolidating the Silk Cut Jaguar Team's complete superiority over all others.

Roger Silman and the team celebrate their success: Eight wins out of ten races, the Teams' Championship, and top four places in the Drivers' Championship. Who could have asked for more?

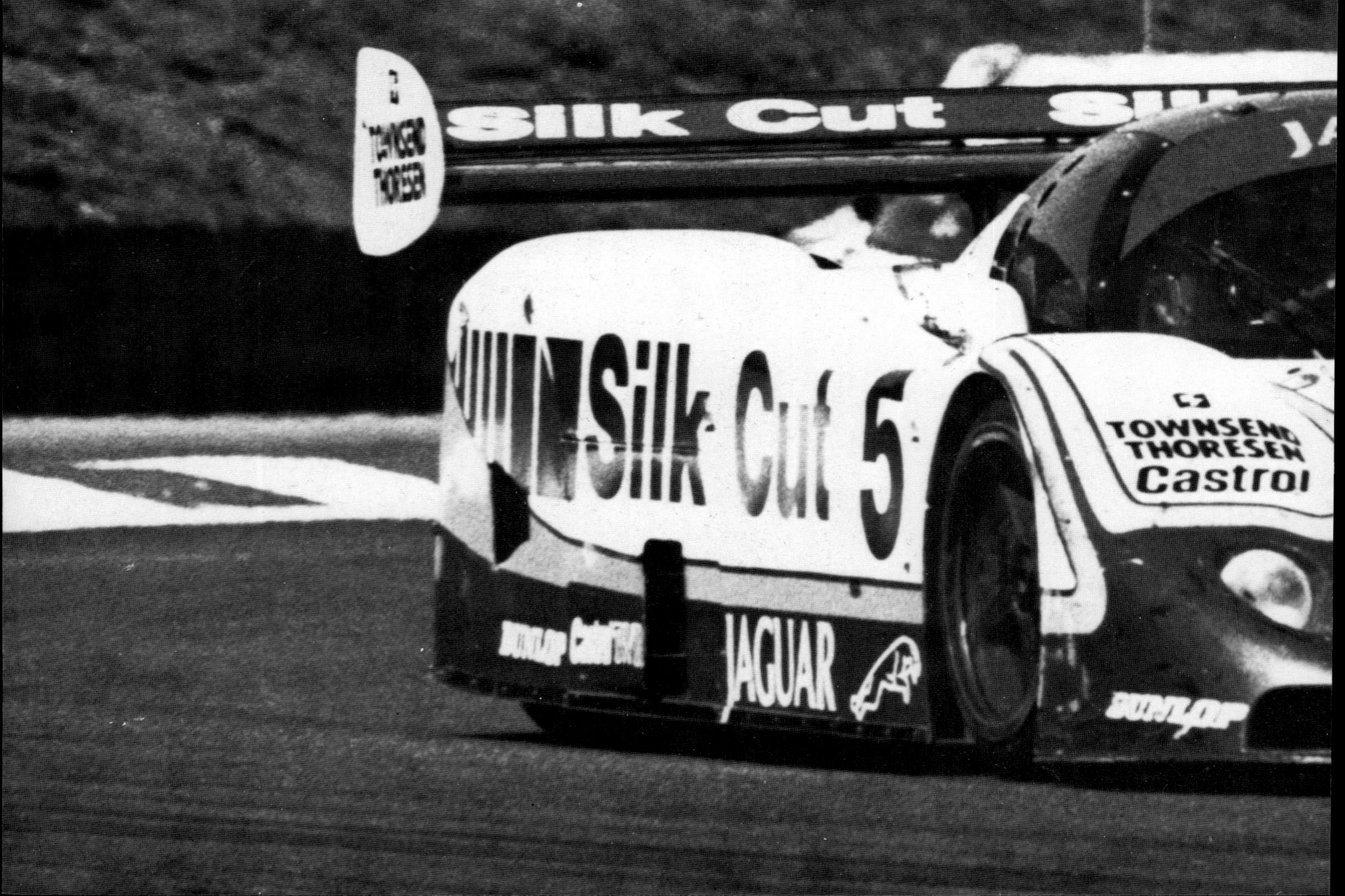

A grand finale: John Watson and Jan Lammers on the Fuji podium with World Champion Raul Boesel *(left)* and Johnny Dumfries. Third place went to Mike Thackwell *(right)* and Mauro Baldi, whose Britten-Lloyd 962C was the most highly developed Porsche to challenge the Jaguars, and the only privately-run car to win a world championship race (Norisring) during 1987.

5

JAGUAR RACING TODAY & TOMORROW

Southgate Plus Silman Spell Success

Group C's pioneering Jaguar XJR-6, the World Championship-winning XJR-8, and their successor the XJR-9 are closely related members of one family: the Walkinshaw-Southgate family. Their relationship to the XJR-5 and XJR-7 (of the Tullius-Dykstra family) is only that of younger and very distant cousins; Even their respective Jaguar V12 engines have been developed separately. In 1986, divorce within the American side of the XJR dynasty led to increased responsibility for its British counterpart.

From 1988, Tom Walkinshaw Racing would be responsible for Jaguar's racing programmes worldwide, and there was certainty that the same technology would be shared equally on both sides of the Atlantic, for the benefit of Jaguar and its two primary racing sponsors: Silk Cut (Gallaher International) and Castrol Inc.

Each sponsor had its own 1988 race series to contend: Castrol had turned out to be Jaguar's long-sought-after IMSA GTP partner, while Silk Cut was back in Group C for a third season, to ensure a full-scale defence of Jaguar's world title.

Of course, the Tullius-Dykstra annulment was not the only factor to make a single contracted Jaguar racing team desirable. The speed with which the Walkinshaw-Southgate alliance had borne fruit showed Jaguar's policymakers that TWR's ground was more fertile than Group 44's.

The XJR-6 was designed by Tony Southgate following a meeting with Tom Walkinshaw in the Summer of 1984, soon after Group 44's first

Sir John Egan (right) *with Tom Walkinshaw's right-hand man and team director, Roger Silman.*

Clare Gibson, secretary for Roger Silman's TWR international racing organisation, based at Kidlington near Oxford.

Link man between Coventry and Kidlington, the sponsors and the sanctioning bodies, Jaguar's racing manager Ron Elkins.

Internal PR is important to Jaguar; although the race cars are not made at Browns Lane, the brand loyalty is there. In

abortive Le Mans effort and shortly before Walkinshaw himself was declared European Touring Car race champion with the Group A Jaguar XJ-S. Having defeated the BMW 635CSi in its special territory Walkinshaw now saw an opportunity for Jaguar to beat another of its great market rivals – Porsche – who ruled sports-car racing.

During the winter of 1984/5, there seemed to be a distinct chance that TWR would use the XJR-5 and adapt Jaguar's experimental 48-valve V12 engine. Indeed one of the American cars was painted dark green after the 1984 NEC motor show and tested on at least two UK circuits. Not only did these events help TWR to rule-out the 48-valve engine as too bulky and complex, but they also served as a red herring while proceedings moved quickly but quietly in the Northamptonshire drawing office of Tony Southgate.

Tony Southgate is renowned worldwide as a freelance race car designer of limitless imagination and considerable adaptability. His imagination helps him keep foremost in his mind the importance of a driver's safe-keeping when an accident happens; his adaptability means that he is quick to take up new technology and incorporate it into his designs. In motor racing, technology has to keep mobile, ready to cope with any sudden whim of the keepers of the rule book. A Coventry man, Southgate has worked for or on behalf of many leading race car manufacturers including Lola, Brabham, BRM, Eagle, Lotus, Shadow and

Arrows. In the early 1980s he went into partnership with the well-known fabricator John Thompson; they formed Auto Racing Technology Ltd and their company was to be close to the TWR Jaguar Group C project.

In designing the Group C Jaguar, Southgate's first task was to reduce to a minimum the effect of having to use a very large V12 engine. It had to be used as a stressed member and it had to be installed as far forward as possible, inset into the rear bulkhead of the central 'cell'. To get the weight down as close as possible to the 850 + kg allowed for Group C cars, and yet to meet the self-imposed safety criteria, composite materials were chosen for their many advantages over metals. From the early 1980s, composites have proved their structural virtues. Perhaps the first real test driver was the notoriously accident-prone Andrea de Cesaris, who crashed his largely carbon fibre F1 McLaren MP4 more times during 1981 even than designer John Barnard could recall – yet was apparently still in good health by the last Grand Prix of the season. McLaren worked with Hercules in the USA, whereas Lotus did their own thing. Alfa Romeo worked with a British company: Advanced Composite Technology Ltd, of Heanor in Derbyshire. In 1984, Tony Southgate went to ACT on behalf of TWR and Jaguar.

Mark Knowles, technical sales manager of Advanced Composite Technology, and his colleague Philip Chandler, have been responsible for the continuous development of the XJR-6/8/9 all-composite structure from the very beginning, working closely with Southgate to achieve the best result. 'There is nothing magic about composites': that comment comes from Knowles, who feels that (outside the racing world) there is still a lack of public confidence in the structural strength of carbon fibre used in conjunction with the DuPont material called Kevlar. His company has been supplying the racing industry with composites since the late 1970s, and some 75 per cent of ACT business is still in that field. High energy-absorption in relation to weight is the special property of composite structures, which are also remarkably puncture-proof – a great feature in the case of accidents in which suspension components or their mountings might attempt to enter the cockpit.

The stiffness of the whole structure is exceptional; the only likely disadvantage of fibrous material could be the time needed for curing when

1987, the regular team drivers came to see the works and meet employees.

Dunlop racing tyres are as much a part of Jaguar today as they were in the 1950s, and they are specified for the 1988 XJR-9 teams on both sides of the Atlantic. Dunlop development engineer Bill Mack has served TWR Jaguar Racing since the ETC Group A programme got under way in 1982.

TWR's race engineers in 1987 (left to right) *Alastair McQueen, Car No.4; Eddie Hinckley, Car No.5; and Ken Page, Car No.6 (Silverstone and Le Mans).*

Raul Boesel (29), the brilliant Brazilian, winner of five of 1987's ten Sports-Prototype World Championship races – and a true champion. (Andrew Whyte photos)

Jaguar versus Porsche: that was the story of 1987. Seen side by side at the Norisring are the year's most-developed Porsche 962 (Baldi/Palmer) which won the event and the Jaguar XJR-8 of Jan Lammers who led for a while. Behind them is the 'Supercup' Porsche of Hans-Joachim Stuck. Although this race and Le Mans were won by Porsches, the other eight went to Jaguar to give the marque its first-ever World Championship. (Jaguar/Malcolm Bryan photos)

Le Mans 1987: All three Silk Cut Jaguars are in the leading bunch at the start and, at a later stage, the prospects of an XJR-8 victory would still look highly favourable. (Andrew Whyte photo)

The new chicane at Le Mans proved a useful safety feature in 1987 when Win Percy (inset) experienced the horror of a high speed accident on the Mulsanne Straight which no amount of work will ever make safe. (Andrew Whyte photos)

New-style Le Mans: The sole surviving XJR-8 rushes through the new chicane, towards the end of the 1987 event.

Despite its dangers, the long Mulsanne Straight has always been part of the fascination of Le Mans (Andrew Whyte photo)

Raising a smile towards the end of the race are Tom Walkinshaw and Graham Whitehead (chatting to John Egan) . . . and Allan Scott (TWR power unit king) and Mike Dale (mastermind of Jaguar's North American racing programme)

Le Mans is an emotional experience. 'Go for it, lads': that was the message from the fans throughout the 1987 race, and the Jaguar folk in the pits took heart from it.

Fifth place was Jaguar's best result at Le Mans for 25 years; but from the crowd's response at the end it could have been mistaken for outright victory, the motor-racing goal which – more than any other – Jaguar wanted to score once again.

The decider: Silk Cut Jaguar became the World Champion Team at the *Nueue Nürburgring* on 30 August 1987. After a startline muddle (caused by Baldi's BLR Porsche almost stalling) the order as the field dived for the first corner was; Ludwig (Joest Porsche), Cheever (Jaguar), Mass (Brun Porsche), Thackwell (Sauber-Mercedes), and Lammers (Jaguar), chased by a host of Porsche 962s. Despite a one-minute penalty, the Cheever/Boesel XJR-8 scored a decisive victory for Jaguar. (Malcolm Bryan photo)

Main picture and inset: Not a success for Jaguar in 1985 or 1986, the Brands Hatch 1000 km race was a crucial event of 1987. Baulked by Mauro Baldi (Britten-Lloyd Porsche), Raul Boesel (No. 4 Jaguar) spun off but, with John Nielsen, he recovered to win the race. Boesel's car is seen about to get the chop from Baldi's and refuelling in the pits later on. (Ian Wagstaff photos)

In 1988, Jaguar sought to defend its World Title and win Le Mans with an even stronger challenge by its latest Southgate creations, now designated 'XJR-9'. Run by Tom Walkinshaw Racing, the Jaguar programme was promised new strength in the form of a 6-litre IMSA GTP version, sponsored by Castrol Inc. The first two IMSA XJR-9s are seen during their successful winter trials at Daytona, driven mainly by Jan Lammers and John Nielsen. TWR's American Jaguar team was to be run by Tony Dowe. (Hal Crocker/Unicorn photos)

Pieces of 8: *Kevin Lee is best known for his pit-stop and signal organisation. He is seen in his Kidlington office with a 'trophy' left behind in Belgium by John Nielsen, who had come so close to the barrier that he hit his own signalling board with the tail of his XJR-8.*

TWR Jaguar team manager Paul Davis with the first XJR-9, Autumn 1987, shortly before its engine was fitted. Note handy hatch in sill, for fuel-line accessibility.

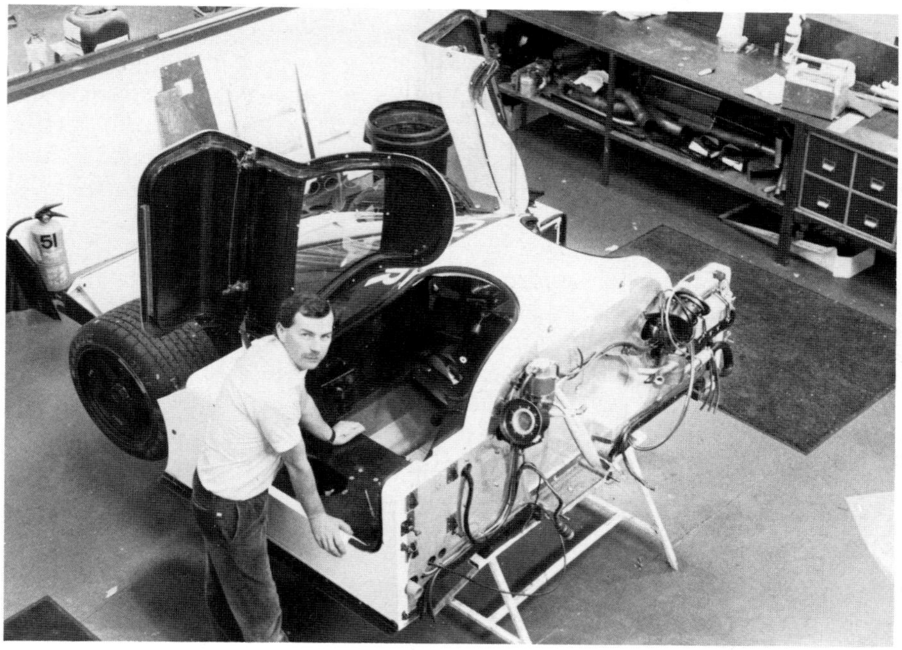

bonding areas back together after, say, a minor practice crash. (There were two such accidents to the same car at Spa-Francorchamps in 1987 – but it did go on to win!).

The suspension of the Southgate cars is fully-independent, featuring magnesium alloy hub carriers, and at the rear the dampers and brake units are kept within the wheels so as to permit the widest possible venturi tunnels. These tunnels are essential to the downforce upon which the car relies for its high cornering speeds. The Jaguar had the greatest downforce of any sports-car; a new rule for 1988 was to limit the venturi height in Group C cars to a maximum of 28 cm, and this was related to a larger flat-bottom area than had been required previously. There are limits to the forces that components will take, and hubs and wheel bearings are among the many that were strengthened as the XJR-6 was developed to become the XJR-8. In fact, TWR claimed a total of sixty-four significant changes when the model changed in the winter of 1986-87 – after a season of irritating set-backs and prior to one of virtual domination.

This was what was so remarkable: that the XJR-6; which had looked quite crude as it was rushed into service for the latter part of 1985 and which so *nearly* won many races for 1986, should become so *completely* successful a design by 1987 when the XJR-8 carried almost all before it.

At first, it had been as important to lighten the engine (without endangering its potential as a chassis member) as to seek more power. New Zealander Allan Scott has lived with Jaguar V12 engines since 1981, first in Group A form (with strict limits on engine breathing) and then with the freedom of Group C ahead of him. He rejected the even heavier, experimental 48-valve engine in favour of the well-tried 24-valver, based upon the familiar sohc (per bank) unit created by Walter Hassan and Harry Mundy in the late 1960s, when Jaguar was concerned more with meeting US emission control regulations than with thoughts of motor racing. Yet those two great engineers had a strong background of racing car experience, especially with Coventry Climax Engines Ltd, the company which Jaguar had bought in 1963 and which helped Cooper and Lotus win two world Formula One titles each. (Hassan had first worked with Jaguar, then SS, in 1938. Before that, he had already made fame as a 'Bentley Boy' and as a builder of Brooklands specials. He retired from Jaguar as chief power unit director in 1972.)

The engine for the XJR-6 began life as a 6-litre dry-sump unit with Lucas Micos engine management, later changed to TWR's own Zytek system. For 1986, its capacity went up to 6.3 litres and by 1987 it had gone up to nearly 7 litres, with an output of over 700 bhp. The race record throughout 1987 showed that Allan Scott's determination to put reliability at a premium had met with the desired results, although valve spring breakage remained an occasional problem.

Fuel consumption (restricted to 510 litres in 1000 km Group C races, with other maxima for other distances) needed careful monitoring, just as in F1 racing. The drivers found the Zytek computer very accurate. One of the biggest improvements for 1987, however, was the system for picking up every last drop of fuel. The 1986 championship had been lost due to recurring misfires, or engines cutting out completely due to apparent starvation – only to be found, afterwards, NOT to have run dry. There was a single fuel tank for 1987 (instead of three separate ones) and a new type of collector. Fuel pressure and temperature became less of a problem, but access to fuel lines was improved all the same.

Unlike the turbocharged opposition, the atmospheric fuel-injected Jaguar engine had no 'instant elixir', like a boost pressure control. It did have a mixture-richness control, however, which could be a help in certain conditions. In Belgium, Eddie Cheever lost a number of places early on, after an electronic fault richened the mixture on one cylinder bank.

Much improved access to the engine bay made pit-work – emergency and otherwise – much simpler in 1987. There is no substitute for experience, and Roger Silman – director of TWR Jaguar Racing since the Group C project began – has proved this in full measure. Few Jaguar Group C racing lessons of a mechanical kind have had to be learned twice.

Allan Scott, manager of TWR's racing engine division. His chief engine builders in 1987 were Charles Bamber, Glen Barber, Peter Grace and Steve Gray. The other engine specialists were Matthew Norris, Neil Peters, Grant Rushton, and Chris Wood – plus Andrew Penny on a youth training scheme. Brian Sheridan was to be in charge of the new engine shop of TWR Inc. in the USA.

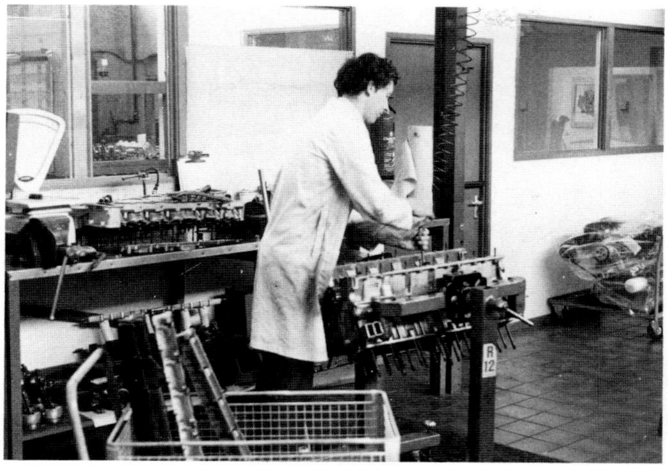

These pictures give a glimpse of the cleanliness of the TWR engine shop. The Scott-modified Jaguar V12 engine for 1987 was producing about 720 reliable bhp at 7000 rpm, and 600 lb ft of torque. Scott's aim is total reliability, and the progress since the Group C project began has been prodigious. He looked at the 48-valve engine (see first colour pages) *in 1984 and 1985 – but at decision-making time he plumped for the regular 24-valve unit as a basis. 'Looking back, I think we did the right thing,' is Scott's view.*

Walter Hassan, seen here at Le Mans in 1987 (where he had first been more than sixty years earlier, as a 'Bentley Boy'), is the father of Jaguar's 24-valve V12 road engine, which Allan Scott has come to admire.

Jaguar V12 racing engine in the Kidlington engine shop, now much lighter than it used to be – but still pretty heavy.

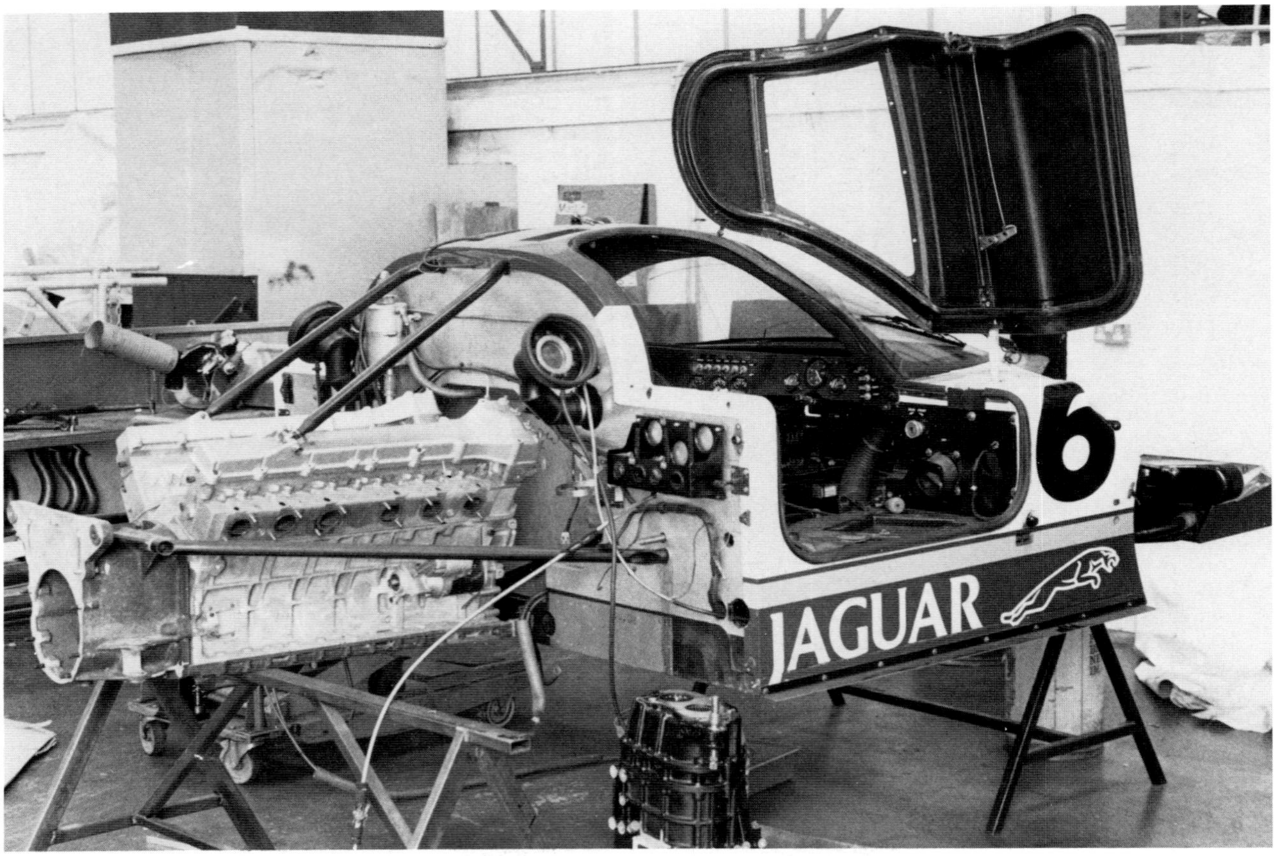

Weight-saving is less of a problem than it was, since the minimum weight figures have been achieved, and Scott makes sure he does nothing to jeopardise the V12's strength as a stressed member of the car.

Scott has lightened many non-stressed engine components by using different materials; but quality and reliability are paramount. Fuel temperature and pick-up problems were largely cured in 1987, and the incidence of broken valve springs was much reduced. The oil system is, incidentally, one third of the weight of that of the XJR-5. This neat little flywheel is a nice example of Scott's attention to detail.

Racer's rear suspension and brake disc in close-up at Kidlington, where the TWR Jaguars are built. However, with Jaguar's own £50 million engineering facility at Whitley, Coventry, becoming fully operational in 1988, TWR could save itself a lot of trouble by testing components there. Another example of Jaguar's engineering resources helping TWR was a special rig for bedding-in brake pads. Such services were organised by Peter Dodd, the Jaguar engineer working closest to TWR on a day-to-day basis.

Roger Silman, Andy Scriven, and Clive Parker discuss the newly arrived second XJR-9 centre-section, with modified engine bay and improved component accessibility (late 1987).

Two more angles on the second XJR-9 'tub'. The day it arrived from Advanced Composite Technology Ltd – a key organisation in the development of composites, which are showing their advantages over traditional aluminium structures more and more. The Jaguar XJR-6/8/9 structure makes full use of all their positive features.

Latest (XJR-9) composites cockpit, photographed at Donington, ACT's previous experience included the structure for the unraced 1983 Nimrod-Aston Martin.

Roger Silman's racing career began with fabrication work for Len Terry in 1967. In 1971 he became chief fabricator for March, then moved to Shadow to master the art of the race mechanic. The natural step was into racing management, and in 1980 his calm and efficient manner (as manager of the Toleman F2 team) was noted by Tom Walkinshaw, who was then sharing premises at Kidlington, Oxford. Walkinshaw asked Silman to join him and eventually, in early 1984, he did so. It is not illogical to suppose that Walkinshaw had told Silman privately that he intended to break out of Group A racing; touring car racing had not been Silman's scene, though his work for TWR undoubtedly helped ease the burden of management sufficiently to let Walkinshaw concentrate upon becoming the European champion touring car driver.

When it came to Group C, however, Walkinshaw – though sorely tempted – never made the mistake of driving his new Jaguar race cars. He forced aside the natural desire to prove himself in this sphere – after all, he had proved himself in so many others – and it can be assumed that the total competence and skilled diplomacy of Roger Silman had something to do with that. Silman, who was made a board director of TWR in 1987, is respected as much by his own team as by Jaguar's management and by the drivers.

Photographed by Malcolm Bryan at Donington Park in Autumn 1987, the engine bay of the XJR-9. Accessibility is an important feature. The Jaguar's engine is much more convenient than the Porsche's when it comes to making space for air-tunnels.

Apart from the fact that several of them have a strong desire to get into Formula One, or to return if they have been there before, the drivers generally enjoy the atmosphere of Group C (and IMSA GTP) racing. Some of them have driven other makes, notably Porsche, and all are full of praise for the work of Southgate, Silman, their regular car managers Eddie Hinckley and Alastair McQueen, and the whole team.

Johnny Dumfries joined the team in late 1987, and shared a win and a runner-up slot with Raul Boesel in the last two races. Dumfries had driven for the best of the opposition only a few weeks earlier, and his views on the three leading C1 cars of 1987 was well worth hearing.

Johnny Dumfries (talking to Sir John Egan and Ron Elkins at Francorchamps) had had recent experience not only of the Porsche 962 but of the impressive Sauber-Mercedes (right) before joining the Silk Cut Jaguar Team in September 1987.

The Japanese remained on the fringe of Group C racing, appearing in force only at Le Mans and Fuji – but a more concerted effort would add further to sports-car variety.

Now for 1988: The IMSA XJR-9 is prepared for its late 1987 tests at Donington Park, where John Watson rated its handling and track behaviour very highly.

The Jaguar XJ13 never raced but, now more than 20 years old, it has become a familiar sight in Le Mans demonstrations.

He drove the Swiss-built Sauber-Mercedes at Le Mans and, briefly, at the Nürburgring. 'It has a lot of horsepower and terrific torque, yet it doesn't feel turbo-ish. The Michelins feel good, too. A full season with sufficient cars: that's what is needed. Mercedes are taking a lot more interest behind the scenes now; I'm sure the Sauber is going to be a force to be reckoned with.'

As for his Porsche experiences, Dumfries had more praise for the pit crew than the car in the case of his IMSA-winning drive at Road America – but he found the Dyson 962 extremely powerful. Of the Britten-Lloyd car, sponsored by Liqui Moly, he had this to say: 'At Brands Hatch it was exceptional, and I admire their manager, Dave Price, who got me my 1984 F3 championship. This Porsche is very different from any other Porsche: very rigid, very sensitive, very fast – and beautifully balanced, with superb brakes.'

Dumfries was driving the XJR-6 for the first time when we talked in Belgium; in fact he had just damaged it, but not too badly for it to be raced next day: 'I find it more nervous than the other Group C cars, more like a single-seater. It doesn't feel as quick as the others but of course it is. It seems happy to brake later and turn in quicker than the others, but the Porsche is a bit better coming out of corners.'

By 1988, Group C had come of age, despite the constant feeling of instability, generated by a politically-motivated governing body.

Porsche had been ousted from its pedestal by Jaguar; and was sure to fight back. Racing is in Porsche's blood; and Porsche still retained its superiority at Le Mans and in IMSA GTP racing – the two areas where Jaguar would be making a special effort with the 1988 XJR-9.

Mercedes were doing more than just dipping their toe in the water. Clearly they wanted a bigger slice of the action, and looked like getting it (through Peter Sauber).

Jaguar had won its championship; now it was more anxious than ever to win again at Le Mans, where it had made its name. With Silk Cut, Castrol, TWR, and Tony Southgate's XJR-9LM perhaps it would do it? (*And* win in America, too?)

Porsche; Mercedes; Jaguar – three of the great names of motordom. Yet few people could have thought, only a few years earlier, that the British marque would be capable of returning to such dizzy heights, of taking on the world's best, and winning.

The Southgate Jaguars

In its earlier heydays, Jaguar raced only front-engined cars. In the mid 1960s, however, it did make one experimental mid-engined car, XJ13; but with the big mergers (BMH and British Leyland) the idea was dropped.

The XJR-5/7 was mid-engined, too; it was of all-American design. The first all-British mid-engined design to win races for Jaguar was the XJR-6, and it was followed by the 1987 championship-winning XJR-8. Further derivatives, for IMSA GTP and Group C racing, were introduced for 1988 under the general designation XJR-9.

The XJR-6, XJR-8 and XJR-9, designed by Tony Southgate and built by Tom Walkinshaw Racing Ltd for Jaguar and its sponsors, are described briefly on the following pages.

The XJR-6

After testing an XJR-5 in Britain, TWR discarded the notion of adapting it for Group C or of racing it in any form at Le Mans – although there were entries for extra Jaguars in 1985's provisional 24-hour race entry list.

Tom Walkinshaw had approached Tony Southgate, the Northamptonshire-based freelance race car designer, in the summer of 1984, when Jaguar was about to be refloated as a fully independent company. He was about to become European Touring car race champion and knew that the XJ-S had completed its planned task for Jaguar in Group A racing. He was itching to see his organisation move on to even greater heights, preferably in parallel with Jaguar's own ascendancy.

Aside from personal reasons (and provided there would be cash to generate the project), there was a good case for considering a completely new design. The chief argument was that the XJR-5 had been built to a 950 kg formula, whereas Group C permitted cars to be as light as 850 kg. The Jaguar V12 engine in all its forms is bulky and relatively heavy. Southgate's achievement was to create such a light car, by using composite material (carbon fibre/Kevlar) for the driver's compartment. Initially, however, the car's weight was still around 900 kg.

The XJR-6 was due to race at Hockenheim in July 1985, but in fact made its bow in Canada on 11 August. The event was the Budweiser 1000 km race at Mosport, and Martin Brundle made a sensational start, leading until Lap 10. Then the two works Porsches went past and, soon afterwards, Brundle retired with a broken wheel-bearing – a function of the enormous

One of several XJR-6 tail configurations tried out at Le Mans practice day, May 1986.

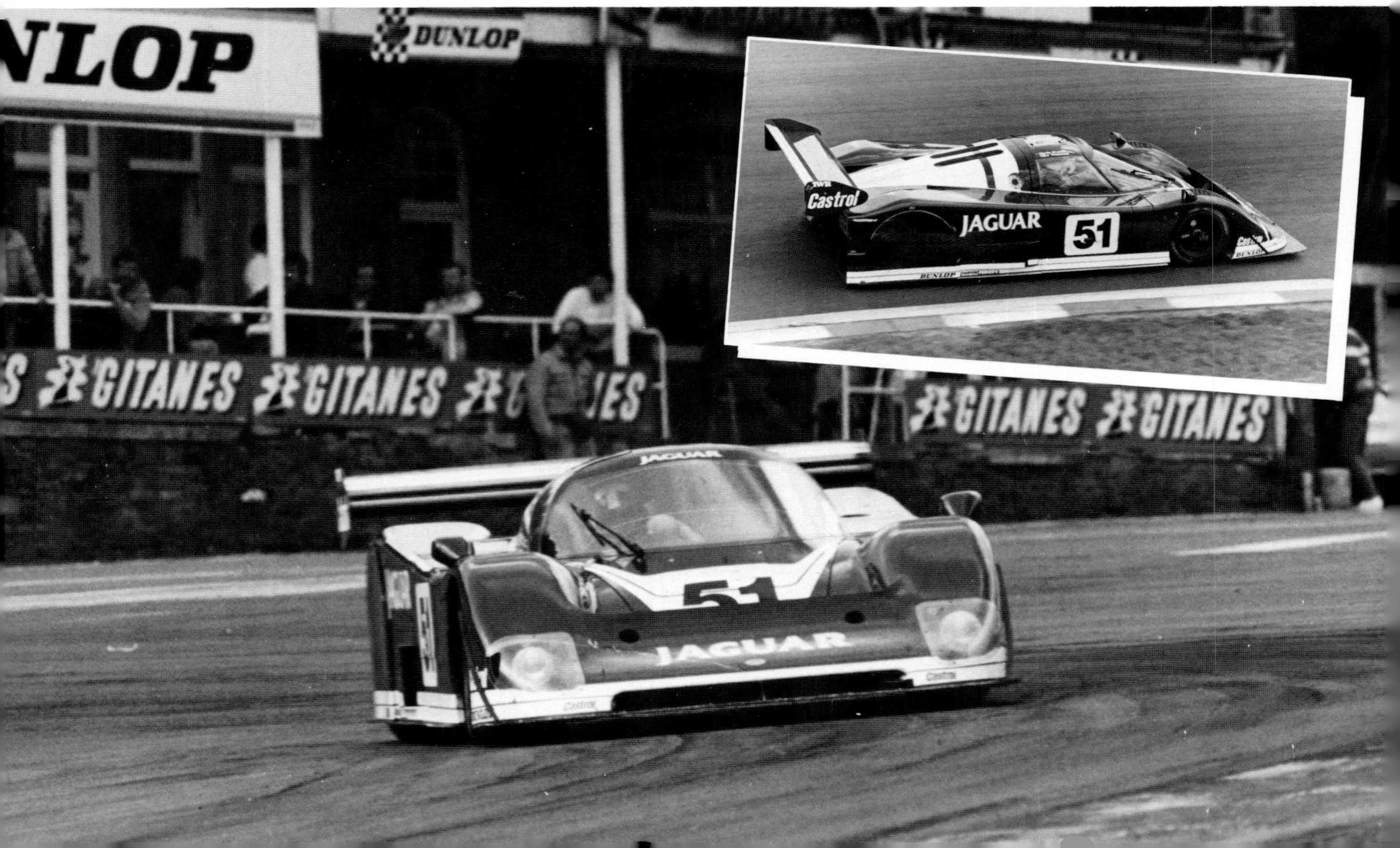

The Brundle/Thackwell XJR-6 en route to fifth place at Spa-Francorchamps in 1985. This was the Southgate-designed car's second race, and its first public appearance in Europe.

Two examples of the XJR-6 in 1986 Silk Cut colours, sandwiching a Porsche during the Belgian 1000 km race.

downforce. However, he shared the driving of a second car with Jean-Louis Schlesser and Mike Thackwell to finish third. At the end of the year an XJR-6 came second at Shah Alam (Kuala Lumpur).

Two XJR-6s were run in World Championship races throughout 1986 and there was an unsuccessful three-car entry at Le Mans. This was the first 'Silk Cut' season. A number of niggling car problems plus several driver errors, meant that only two races were won: The Kouros 1000 km, race at Silverstone, where Eddie Cheever and Derek Warwick shared the driving, and the German Supercup final at the Neue Nürburgring where Cheever beat Porsche men Hans-Joachim Stuck and Klaus Ludwig.

The most exciting Group C race of 1986 was the Belgian event, however. A Silk Cut Jaguar failed *by less than a second* to beat one of Walter Brun's Porsches after 1000 km; it made the difference between winning and losing the world title. The same could be said of any one of a number of 1986 incidents *(see first colour section).*

The Jaguar XJR-8

So many improvements to the XJR-6 were incorporated after the 1986 season that the Silk Cut Jaguar Team cars for 1987 were designated XJR-8. From the start there was also an XJR-8LM specification (for Le Mans).

It was to be a great season, the success of which has led to the publication of this book. At the start, the XJR-6 received a Design Council Award, a tribute to Tony Southgate's ability to create a special-purpose car from modern materials, and make it a race winner against the best sports-prototypes in the world. Southgate is a designer's designer.

The achievements of the XJR-8, in winning eight of the ten 1987 World series races from the all-powerful Porsches, are recorded individually, on other pages. The victories were at Jarama, Jerez, Monza, Silverstone, Brands Hatch, Nürburgring, Spa-Francorchamps and Fuji. Only the marathon of Le Mans and a sprint at the Norisring eluded the XJR-8. It was almost as if Jaguar had achieved a Porsche-like monopoly. Porsche does not rest on its laurels. In the winter of 1987-88, TWR and Tony Southgate were not going to do so either. Already an XJR-9 was on the way . . .

Jaguar XJR-8 in what Tony Southgate called 'sprint' trim: to him, even a 1000 km race is a sprint, compared with Le Mans. This picture shows the car as 'artworked' for Jaguar's own World Championship advertising.

Jaguar XJR-8LM on test in early 1987. One was raced at Silverstone and three at Le Mans.

The Jaguar XJR-9

XJR-9 was the general designation for the British built V12-powered sports-prototypes to be raced in 1988 as a 6-litre GTP car *or* as a Group C car. It was the latest version of Tony Southgate's brilliant design, previously seen as the XJR-6 (1985-6) and the XJR-8 (1987).

The IMSA GTP version was announced in New York on 19 October 1987. Having been given preliminary tests by John Watson in Britain, it was

John Watson tests the IMSA GTP XJR-9 at Donington Park,

late 1987, photographed by Malcolm Bryan.

XJR-9 at its public launching in New York's Central Park, Autumn 1987. (In Europe, the Group C version would still carry the Silk Cut banner in 1988.)

As with the XJR-8, the XJR-9 has front-hinged doors. (The XJR-6 had less-satisfactory 'gull wings'.)

taken to Daytona for a full test programme. Jan Lammers and John Nielsen were among the drivers.

Sponsored by Castrol, and managed by a US-based TWR company under Tony Dowe's management, the XJR-9 was to take over from the XJR-7 as Jaguar's official US race car. (However, it was thought that the Group 44 XJR-7 would still be seen in 1988 as a private venture.)

The XJR-9 for Group C and the XJR-9LM Le Mans cars would defend their World title under the Silk Cut banner.

It remained to be seen just how many more seasons would allow the XJR-6/8/9 to evolve further, for the potential stability of race regulations was under constant threat. Whatever the future may hold, the intervention of Jaguar, TWR and Tony Southgate in the sports-prototype domain of the 1980s must go down in history as a brilliant success, on a par with the achievements of Ford in the 1960s and Porsche itself in the 1970s. A win at Le Mans for the XJR-9 or one of its successors would complete that picture . . .

1985-1988 JAGUAR XJR-6/8/9

Group C & IMSA Camel GT

Engine: Jaguar 60-degree V12; two valves per cylinder; one chain-driven camshaft for each bank of cylinders; engine, load-bearing and centrally mounted.

Capacity:	6 litres for XJR-6, increasing to 6.3 and 6.5 litres in 1986, then 6.9 litres for XJR-8 (1987). New IMSA version for 1988, restricted by rules to 6 litres, designated XJR-9. Various outputs in 600-700 hp range.
Materials:	Aluminium alloy cylinder block and heads; pistons forged in aluminium alloy; connecting rods in steel and titanium; seven-bearing crankshaft in forged steel.
Fluids:	Water cooling through front-mounted aluminium radiator; oil system incorporates dry sump; fuel/air system features fuel injection and electronic management, inlet being via individual injectors drawing air through a single air filter (inlet in 'V').

Chassis/Body: Advanced Composites monocoque in carbon fibre/Kevlar, with steel-tube supports for engine which is a stressed member.

Body:	Lightweight composite and glass-fibre, with carbon-fibre reinforcement. Underside has regulation flat surfaces and ground-effect air ducts as permitted by Group C and IMSA regulations. (Lower venturi height and bigger reference surface demanded for 1988 Group C cars.) Two doors, top-hinged for XJR-6, front-hinged for XJR-8/9. Aerodynamics include enclosed rear wheels, except on Le Mans cars from 1987. (Le Mans cars also have less ground-effect and body/wing modifications specially for that circuit.)
Front suspension:	Wide-base fabricated wishbones actuating pushrods to spring/damper units mounted horizontally at centre-line of car; magnesium alloy hub carriers.
Rear suspension:	Magnesium alloy uprights and steel coil springs. Shock absorbers and brake discs housed within wheels, to permit maximum air-duct width.
Wheels/tyres:	Latest Dunlop Denloc Kevlar/rubber tyre technology and 17-inch diameter wheels on 1988 XJR-9. (XJR-6/8 had 19-inch rears.)
Transmission:	March five-speed (and reverse) gearbox with straight-cut gears, via hydraulically-operated AP Racing triple disc clutch.

Dimensions:

Weight:	890 kg reducing to regulation minimum of 850 kg for XJR-8 in Group C (1987). New IMSA version of XJR-9 meets IMSA 900 kg minimum requirement.
Fuel capacity:	100 litres for Group C; XJR-9 for IMSA incorporates 120-litre accommodation as allowed.
Length/width:	4.8 metres and 2.0 metres.

Designer/Constructor: Tony Southgate/Tom Walkinshaw Racing Ltd.

Postscript: Jaguar & IMSA

For 1988, TWR and Jaguar were not only continuing for a third season as the Silk Cut Jaguar Team in WSC racing; they were instigating a completely separate operation in North America for the IMSA Camel GTP series, with Castrol sponsorship.

The USA has played a big part in the return of Jaguar to racing – a sixth Le Mans victory always being the ultimate goal. Not many marques have proved themselves capable of winning Le Mans. There are other pickings along the way, however. Both Group 44 and TWR have scored notable successes every year since they became involved in their sports-prototype race programme. The chief difference between the teams is that TWR was more successful, more often, thereby attracting more sponsorship money. As their relative strengths and weaknesses were compared – with a view to creating a single, co-ordinated Jaguar race programme worldwide – TWR was the natural choice.

Had Group 44 been an expanding organisation, moving with the times, it might have got the sponsorship necessary to help fund a full-scale programme. After all, Group 44 had instigated the 'XJR' series of modern Jaguar racers. But despite a lot of effort in the USA, particularly during 1986, no major backer was to be found for the popular team created by Robert Tullius in the early 1960s.

Bob Tullius had raced Triumph sports cars in SCCA events, frequently winning races and championships. These production car races had been truly amateur in the 1950s, but in the 1960s Tullius – perhaps more than anyone – brought in a professional element. In fact he was setting a trend, in those days, with his Quaker State Oil sponsorship deal and his smart green-on-white livery which the Group 44 team retains to this day. ('Group 44' was named after his own racing number.) There is hardly a branch of motor racing these days that does not rely on sponsorship of some kind for its very existence.

By the 1970s, Group 44 was closely associated with British Leyland Motors Inc., USA, and in particular with up-and-coming BL sales executive Michael Dale – an expatriate Briton and a sports-car race winner himself, with a number of SCCA successes to his (and his Sprite's) credit. By this time, Jaguar had begun to change. Although it had been part of British Leyland from the outset (1968) Jaguar, initially, had kept a good deal of its character and autonomy. After the retirement of Sir William Lyons in 1972, however, the pressure to integrate the company fully into BL* became stronger. Jaguar's founder had gone to the USA for a final pre-retirement sales mission, chiefly to launch the new V12 engine, in 1971. That timing fitted-in with the retirement of the man who had run Jaguar Cars Inc. for many years, Johannes Eerdmans, whose business was naturally integrated into that of Austin, Morris, MG, Rover, Triumph, *et al,* under the presidency of Graham Whitehead.

Following the first international crisis-of-confidence over fuel, the motor markets of the world entered a rough patch in late 1973. Jaguar's famous E-type sports car was a major sufferer, and Bob Tullius was called

upon to make a racer of it. As Jaguar Cars Inc.'s public relations manager, Michael Cook, explains: 'The racing effort in 1974 was calculated to assist E-type sales which were dropping off fast, despite the knowledge that the model was going out of production. The 1975 season and the transition year of 1976 were indications of how racing had become part of the corporate marketing strategy for Jaguar. As we looked unhappily at the non-sports-car image of the XJ-S, we tried to counter it with a Trans Am racing program.'

At a time when Jaguar in Britain was running into real trouble – without a proper management structure, or any control over BL's abortive ETC programme – the unexpected appearance of the controversial XJ-S as a race-winner in the USA was a wonderful fillip for the marque, despite BL overtones in its presentation. 'Thundering Elegance' was the ambiguous-sounding slogan of the day, and Tullius won his Trans Am category in both 1977 and 1978. In the latter year, the Group 44 XJ-S also gave Jaguar the manufacturer's title. Ironically, manufacturing problems in Britain were restricting production of all Jaguars to an uneconomic level, and so Group 44 switched to racing Triumphs again – this time in the IMSA GT category.

Sports-car racing and Jaguar grew up together in the USA. This picture captures the mood of the early post-war years, and shows two favourite British marques – Jaguar and MG – leading Allards, Aston Martins and the Chinetti Ferrari away from a Le Mans-type start. The event is the very first Sebring endurance race, the brainchild of Alec Ulmann, and run from 3 pm to 9 pm on New Year's Eve 1950/51. It was a handicap event, won by the speck at the extreme left – a tiny American Crosley Hotshot. In 1952, Sebring became a 12-hour race, and a year later it made history as the first World Sports Car Championship race of all. Sebring doesn't look all that different today.

Phil Hill gives the Jaguar XK120C its first US race victory on 6 September 1952. The car was owned by West Coast importer Chuck Hornburg and the event was the Sheldon Cup on the Elkhart Lake street circuit, soon to be replaced by 'Road America'.

From 1955 to 1963, Briggs Cunningham raced Jaguars and Jaguar-powered Listers, often with great success. He sponsored the works D-type which won at Sebring in 1955, and acquired his own blue-and-white long-nose D-type for that year's Le Mans. Afterwards it was taken to the USA, and Sherwood Johnston was immediately successful with it; Johnston became the 1955 SCCA Class C Modified national champion – a title which Walter Hansgen would take for the next four years, mostly driving Cunningham's cars. Cunningham had a good rapport with Jaguar, and borrowed a number of race cars from Coventry. The 'D' (seen here after one of Johnston's wins) stayed in the Cunningham collection.

After over a decade without competitive equipment, the marque returned to the sport in 1974 with the V12-engined E-type in SCCA Class B Production racing. Bob Tullius, seen here, became national champion in this category in 1975. Retrospectively, this car can be considered as 'XJR-1'.

By 1980 Triumph's days were numbered. So, it seemed were Jaguar's. However, it had been apparent for two years that (Sir) Michael Edwardes was the first BL chief executive to appreciate that you need more than a marque *name* if you are to maintain a worthwhile marque. For Jaguar, his was a prescription of kill or cure; in order to raise morale, improve quality, and step up production to an economic level, Edwardes sought out John Egan, who came to Browns Lane in April 1980. For some months it was touch-and-go, but Egan was soon injecting new life into every aspect of the business. He did not look at motor racing immediately, although in the back of his mind he recalled the great Jaguar Le Mans victories of his schooldays.

When he went to America in the autumn John Egan presented US-based Englishman Fred Baker with the Jaguar Driver of the Year award – an annual trophy, put up by Jaguar for achievements outside the world of big-sponsorship competitions: not that Jaguar was in the big-time – yet (although Tullius had run his first XJ-S in the 1976 IMSA Camel GT finale at

Bob Tullius and his team, Group 44, raced the Jaguar XJ-S in various forms, being particularly successful in SCCA championship events in 1977, 1978, and 1981. Here he leads his then-partner and chief engineer Brian Fuerstenau in the 1978 Trans Am final at Mexico City's Autodromo Ricardo Rodriguez, *which Tullius won.*

The men who masterminded Jaguar's US racing operations between 1974 and 1987 – Robert Tullius and Michael Dale.

Daytona, prior to his two Trans Am seasons). Baker had done a real giant-killing job with an elderly six-cylinder E-type prepared by dealer Lou Fidanza of Eastlake, Ohio: he had won the 1980 SCCA national C-production final at Road Atlanta, beating reigning champion Paul Newman whose Datsun ZX was one of several highly-fancied runners. Egan could see that the relatively high degree of public exposure gained by an obsolete Jaguar must be multiplied several times over, with a new car, and in a bigger arena.

Bob Tullius and Bill Adam had come second and fourth respectively in the 1980 IMSA 'GT' category with their Group 44 Triumph TR8s; but the overall IMSA champion was John Fitzpatrick (Porsche 935): and *overall* victory is what has always interested Jaguar. For a while, it looked as if Tullius would close down his racing workshops and take up some new line of business – maybe in historic sports cars. But then came a change of IMSA ragulations, designed to stop the Porsche monopoly, and it was not long before Egan was talking to Mike Dale and discovering that he, too, dreamed of bringing the name Jaguar back to the highest echelons of sports-car racing – meaning 'Le Mans' and whatever paths might lead to victory there again.

For 1981, as a gap-filling exercise, Group 44 was given the go-ahead to race a tubular-framed V12-engined XJ-S lookalike in the main SCCA Trans Am series. Tullius won three of the nine races and was second in the championship. Meanwhile Brian Redman's Lola-Chevrolet dominated IMSA's new 'GTP' series – the series which had caught Dale's eye. The gap to be filled was that between drawing board and first shakedown trials of Jaguar's own mid-engined GTP car, designed and built in the USA – that is to say, designed by Lee Dykstra and built by Group 44.

Graham Whitehead, British President of Jaguar's North American subsidiary, announced the official return of Jaguar to racing in January 1982:

'The United States is now recognised by Jaguar for what it is . . . the largest potential market for Jaguar products in the world. Our moves are their moves, and our input is acknowledged as essential to the future success of the company.'

Mike Cook re-emphasised that theme just six seasons later, when the Group 44 Jaguar liaison was coming to an end: 'The commitment to IMSA Camel GTP racing was much greater than the 1974 (E-type) and 1977 (Trans Am XJ-S) decisions. It involved a tremendous amount of money and a return to international class racing where everything had to be one hundred per cent from design to driver selection and team operation. Naturally, there was participation in this decision from both sides of the Atlantic, but it was generated here.' (Cook was speaking in his New Jersey office.) 'John Egan's perception that victory at Le Mans would greatly enhance the image of the company assisted the decision and is still a goal of the program . . .', Cook added; and it must have passed through his mind, and the minds of many others, that strength in numbers is a major factor at Le Mans from the manufacturer's point of view. Would Castrol sponsor a car, or cars, as an extra Group C 'package' to support the Silk Cut Jaguar Team at Le Mans during the new sponsor's three-year IMSA contract fo Jaguar Cars Inc? From TWR's point of view there would be merit in that notion, for, on several occasions, Tom Walkinshaw had expressed his preference NOT to be a supplier (*à la* Porsche) to customer teams – *Ecurie Ecosse* being an early discoverer of this fact.

Lee Dykstra, designer of the XJR-5 and XJR-7. The crunch for Group 44 and its relationship with Jaguar (who had hired Dykstra) occurred at the time of the 1986 Daytona 24-hour race, when Tullius shut Dykstra out of the Jaguar pit area. Naturally Dykstra severed his connection with the team after that.

An XJR-5 visited Britain for the first time in mid-1983. It was driven at Silverstone by Derek Bell, who reported favourably enough for Group 44 to be given two stabs at Le Mans, in 1984 and 1985.

Road *racing in the USA can mean the swoops of* Road *America or the dives of* Road *Atlanta – and it can mean the wide open spaces of Sebring or the tight confines of real streets, as in downtown Miami, where the XJR-7 of Bob Tullius and Chip Robinson is seen in action in 1986.*

Back in 1982, when Walkinshaw was beginning his Group A Jaguar XJ-S project for Europe, the first American Jaguar (and the first mid-engined Jaguar since the XJ13 of the 1960s) was taking shape in Group 44's new Winchester, Virginia, workshops.

Bob Tullius and Mike Dale should get the credit for initiating the 'XJR' sequence of Jaguar nomenclature, incidentally.

Retrospectively, the first official Jaguar entry in modern motor racing, the 1974-1976 C-production class Group 44 V12 E-type, must be 'XJR-1'. The 1976-77 XJ-S Trans Am car is, therefore, 'XJR-2'; its 1978 successor, 'XJR-3'; and the 1981 tube-frame car 'XJR-4'. That is how the XJR-5 got its name, anyway.

Lee Dykstra, independent Michigan engineer and proprietor of Special Chassis Inc., was already famous for his design work in GTP (for John Paul) and for other race-car categories. His distinctive XJR-5 (styled by off-duty GM folk) was strongly constructed with steel bulkheads, aluminium honeycomb floor, and a sleek glass-fibre semi-monocoque body. Initially, the Jaguar engine was stated to be a 5.3-litre 525 bhp unit fed by six Weber carburettors. The XJR-5 raced for the first time in the Road America, Wisconsin, 500-miler on 22 August 1982. Driven by Bob Tullius and Bill Adam it came third behind the Porsche 935 turbos of past champion John Fitzpatrick and champion-elect John Paul, Jr.

As with almost any team, Group 44 was to have its share of bad luck during four full years plus two 'part-seasons'. In 1982, the promising start was followed by a couple of crashes. No-one was hurt, but there were no more results to show.

With just one car, Group 44 scored four outright victories in 1983, despite, its car being somewhat underpowered. The Porsche 962 was not yet ready, and the remarkable but shortlived front-engined Mustang GTP was able to score its only GTP victory this year. The other twelve races went to Porsche and March derivatives. Bob Tullius, however, was runner-up to Al Holbert in the series.

Despite a bigger budget and a two-car team, Group 44 managed to score only one victory a year during 1984-5-6; but the team did put up heroic displays at Le Mans in 1984 and 1985, Tullius taking thirteenth place on the latter occasion. An updated version of the Dykstra design named XJR-7 (TWR had taken XJR-6 for its group C car) made its début at Daytona on 1 December 1985, coming fourth. Still it did not match the turbocharged cars on sheer performance although past-champion Brian Redman, who had joined the team in 1984, declared: 'Lee Dykstra has provided us with the best-stopping and best-handling cars in GTP racing'. By now the car had a 6.5-litre engine with Lucas Micos engine management.

Unfortunately, victories were becoming too-thinly spread – due mainly to the Porsche 962 – and there was now friction in the Group 44 camp. It came to a head at Daytona where Tullius surprised his colleagues and everyone else by using security guards to keep unwanted visitors out of the Group 44 pit during the 1986 24-hour race. Even Jaguar PR man Mike Cook was barred – *but,* most obvious of all, designer Lee Dykstra was treated as *persona non grata* by Bob Tullius. It seems that there was difference of opinion over certain XJR-7 design features. Justified or not, such arguments do not show up well on public display. Not surprisingly,

1987 was a crucial year for Jaguar Cars Inc., with the launching of the new XJ40 range in Florida in the spring. It was at about this time that Jaguar took the decision to use TWR for its entire racing programme – Group C and IMSA. The men who implemented the team switch in America were Graham Whitehead (above) *president of Jaguar Cars Inc., and his senior vice-president Mike Dale*.

Castrol and Jaguar join forces for a three-year IMSA programme, starting in 1988. Seen here with the XJR-9 are the principal figures (left to right) *at the October 1987 launch at Central Park's Boathouse Café, New York: Michael Dale, senior vice-president, sales and marketing for Jaguar Cars Inc.; Dr Gerald Owen, director, Development Division, Castrol Limited; Graham Whitehead, president, Jaguar Cars Inc,: John Gardella, vice-president, Castrol Inc; Tom Walkinshaw, head of TWR; Roger Silman, team director TWR European operations; Tony Dowe, TWR Inc's team leader for the USA; and Ian Reed, chief engineer for TWR Inc. – Walkinshaw's new Indiana operation.*

Dykstra (despite being retained by Jaguar) felt he had no option but to leave Group 44.

This personality clash must have sown the seeds of doubt within Jaguar's management in Coventry and in Leonia, New Jersey. There was now a strong feeling that Group C and IMSA GTP regulations were getting closer and closer, and that basically similar cars could be used for both categories. Porsche's 962 had been derived from the 956, specifically for IMSA. There had been a plan at one stage for TWR to adapt the XJR-5 as a Group C car; but politics and weight were among many reasons why Tom Walkinshaw rejected – or persuaded Jaguar to reject – the US design in favour of the one by Tony Southgate.

Another problem in the USA was a continued lack of outside sponsorship. Group 44 had discarded its long-standing agreement of mutual promotion with Quaker Oils after 1983, and it had been small beer before that. The cars looked beautiful, in white, with only the word 'Jaguar' visible apart from the racing numbers ('44' and '04') and strong 'Good Year' embossing on the tyres. The hunt was on, throughout 1986, to find a big backer. Sponsors came close, but no-one signed. The cars looked a million dollars; the teamwork was magnificent; but where was that chequered flag?

Nearly twenty months had passed without a Group 44 victory when success returned in the 1986 Daytona finale. But it was too late by then, Tullius had to face 1987 running only one car, in a limited IMSA programme. Irony of ironies it proved to be a season of good results – two outright victories for the XJR-7, plus the coveted Kodak Copiers $10,000 Top Pit Crew Award for the second year running.

For the 'sudden death play-off' at Del Mar, California, on 25 October 1987, Group 44 was sponsored by a dealer, Performance Jaguar of San Diego. In the race itself, the car ran quite competitively; then mechanical trouble intervened and it dropped to tenth. However, despite their limited season with the car, John Morton and Hurley Haywood were placed eighth and ninth in the championship.

However, in the pit-stop play-off against Derek Bell and new champion Chip Robinson of the Holbert Porsche team, Group 44's crew directed by the legendary Lawton ('Lanky') Foushee broke all records for the simulated pit-stop, which includes changing all four wheels, cleaning the windscreen (covered in transmission fluid) and simulated refuelling with the nozzle in place for a minimum of fifteen seconds. There must be a driver change, and the stopwatch stops when the car has accelerated ten feet forwards. Only five crew members may be in front of the pit wall. For the 1987 final they were Brian Berthold, Pat Hawley, Eric Kent (fuel line), Brian Krem, and Grant Weaver. Their winning time of 17.78 seconds seemed hardly credible. The Holbert Porsche crew took 24.11 seconds. When the Jaguar beat the Porsche to win at Riverside and Palm Beach earlier in the year, the winning margin had been less than the difference between those times. On both occasions Haywood and Morton had done the actual winning, of course, but the disciplined speed of the Group 44 crew did much to equate the performance of their car with the opposition.

The Group 44 work for Jaguar had, in fact, finished back in the summer (indeed, there had also been special sponsorship for the win at Palm Beach). It was in May that TWR's IMSA GTP deal with Jaguar was confirmed, and in July Jaguar Cars Inc. held a no-hard-feelings party for Group 44 at Watkins Glen, where Tullius and Morton drove the XJR-7 for the last time as an official Jaguar entry. It was another heroic battle against all odds, but they did finish, amid spontaneous cheers – for Group 44 had become the heroic underdog.

But in those few short years, Jaguar had gone from rags to riches (no matter what the stockmarkets were doing in late 1987), and the underdog image had been replaced by one of driving ambition – ambition to win in the market place and on the race circuit. Group 44 had always been conscientous and eager as a team, and had performed with credit. The team won races – but not often enough. In the same period (1982 to 1987), Jaguars prepared by TWR had won thirty races; Group 44 had nearly won that many, but it had actually won nine times. This is the Group 44 IMSA GTP victory record:

1983

Road Atlanta	Bob Tullius/Bill Adam (XJR-5)
Lime Rock	Bob Tullius/Bill Adam (XJR-5)
Mosport	Bob Tullius/Bill Adam (XJR-5)
Pocono	Bob Tullius/Doc Bundy (XJR-5)

1984

Miami Brian	Redman/Doc Bundy (XJR-5)

IMSA GTP racing has come closer and closer to Group C – or is it vice versa? John Bishop founded IMSA, and is responsible for the international reputation of its Camel GT series.

1985

Road Atlanta	Brian Redman/Hurley Haywood (XJR-5)

1986

Daytona	Bob Tullius/Chip Robinson (XJR-7)

1987

Riverside	Hurley Haywood/John Morton (XJR-7)
Palm Beach	Hurley Haywood/John Morton (XJR-7)

For 1988, Group 44 was expected to continue to run in some GTP races with the XJR-7, if sponsorship was forthcoming; likewise an Indycar programme for Chip Robinson.

Throughout the summer of 1987, Tom Walkinshaw and Roger Silman – by now a TWR board director – laid their IMSA plans for 1988. Meanwhile Guy Edwards moved among the moguls in search of the right sponsor. Although Castrol had been associated with the Jaguar Group C effort since 1985 in a fairly small way (and would continue the arrangement in 1988), its United States company would be the primary sponsor for the new IMSA project, in conjunction with Jaguar Cars Inc. – both being located just west of New York City, in New Jersey.

The official announcement was made at a function in Central Park, New York, on 19 October 1987 by Graham W. Whitehead and Thomas R. Crane Jr – respective Presidents of Jaguar Cars Inc. and Castrol Inc. – and the program for 1988 would be managed by Michael H. Dale, Jaguar's senior vice-president, sales and marketing, and John S. Gardella, vice-president, automotive sales for Castrol. The cars would be prepared and run by TWR, the racing organisation which had just won the World Sports-Prototype Team Championship for Jaguar. TWR would operate from a base in Valparaiso, Indiana, run by British-born Tony Dowe, previously associated with Carl Haas's Lola racing team and thoroughly familiar with competition in North America. Chief engineer for the team would be Ian Reed, also a Briton turned US resident and fresh from several seasons with the Shierson Indianapolis car team. It was anticipated that the team would employ about 35 people, most of them Americans.

'We have been unique as a manufacturer in world-class racing,' said Dale at the press conference. 'For the past six years, we have fielded a competitive team in the IMSA Camel GTP series without a principal sponsor. It is impossible for a relatively small company to maintain that level of expenditure without assistance and it is difficult to justify devoting such a large percentage of our marketing budget to one area. We are especially pleased with our three-year agreement with Castrol Inc.'

It was just coming up to twenty-five years since Castrol and Jaguar had first collaborated on the race track for a successful long-distance record attempt at Monza, Italy. Although this event was not noted in the press release, both parties emphasised the marketing value they attached to their respective company histories in the field of motor sports. Tom Walkinshaw himself was, as always, much more concerned about the present and the immediate future. He was careful not to under-estimate the new job his team now faced:

'We have earned our spurs in the rest of the world,' he said, 'but we bring no false self-confidence into our IMSA operation. We know that our car is potentially a winner, but we must build a winning team to support it. We'll do that by taking the best managers and mechanics from both sides of the Atlantic. We'll have a British car, but it will be run by a heavily American-orientated team.'

In fact Tony Dowe and Ian Reed had already begun winning their TWR spurs as early as September 1987, when they had taken responsibility for the Silk Cut team's extra XJR-8 in Belgium where a victory for Raul Boesel would make him World Champion. Helped by Brundle and Dumfries, Boesel did win – in 'their' car!

The 1988 car was to be called the XJR-9. John Watson, not normally given to displays of enthusiasm, waxed lyrical about the test laps he had done before the first one was shipped to the United States. Due to the enforced reduction to 6 litres for IMSA, it may have been a little down on power (620 bhp at 7000 rpm, said the release), but Watson found it smoother to drive at racing speeds than the XJR-8.

Jaguar's World Champion, Raul Boesel, with the new XJR-9 in New York, shortly before testing it at Daytona in readiness for the 1988 Camel GTP season.

With a schedule of some twenty-five races (15 IMSA plus 10 Group C), TWR was embarking on its busiest season yet, when this book went to press in January 1988. Full details of Jaguar's plans for that season can be found on Page 24.

By New Year 1988, it was also possible to foresee the future of sports-car racing a little more clearly than before, thanks to some positive advance information on the Group C front, at least until the end of 1990. Perhaps the entrants' desire for stability in the regulations was being heeded, and perhaps – with even more traditional marques taking part, as noted by Peter Falk in his foreword – this branch of the sport would flourish even more in the years ahead. Top drivers, who still cherished the idea of success in Formula One, were discovering that there was pleasure as well as prestige to be found in the world of the sports-prototype. Being associated with a great marque – Porsche, Jaguar, Mercedes-Benz, or Aston Martin, for example – may have had something to do with that. One thing was sure: TWR and Jaguar would be made to earn their laurels more than ever – an exciting era lay ahead as 1988 dawned brightly.